This publication was partially funded by
the Missouri Arts Council

and the Archaeological Institute of America

Studies in
CYPRIOTE ARCHAEOLOGY

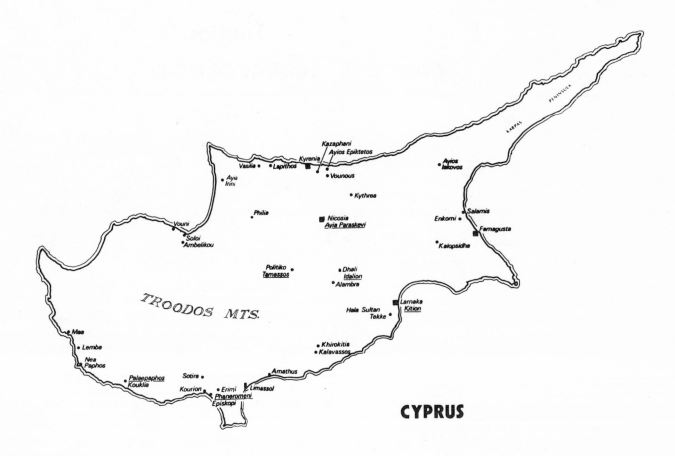

CYPRUS

Studies in

CYPRIOTE ARCHAEOLOGY

Edited by

Jane C. Biers   •   David Soren

Monograph XVIII

Institute of Archaeology, University of California, Los Angeles

Director of Publications: Ernestine S. Elster

Institute of Archaeology,
University of California, Los Angeles
Copyright 1981, by the Regents of the University of California
All rights reserved
ISBN: 0-917956-23-0
Printed in the United States of America

CONTENTS

PART IV. Kourion (continued)

CONTRIBUTORS

Michael Arwe, East Surrey Road, Keene, New Hampshire.

Jane C. Biers, Museum of Art and Archaeology, University of Missouri-Columbia.

Darice Birge, 508 Laurel Lane, Apt. 4, East Lansing, Michigan.

Hillary Browne, 19 West Amherst Road, Cynwd, Pennsylvania.

Diana Buitron, The Walters Art Gallery, Baltimore.

James R. Carpenter, Department of Classical Studies, Kent State University.

Stephen C. Glover, Department of Art History and Archaeology, University of Missouri-Columbia.

Ellen Herscher, 3309 Cleveland Ave, NW, Washington D.C.

Vassos Karageorghis, Department of Antiquities, Nicosia, Cyprus.

Susan Kromholz, PSC Box 100, APO San Francisco, California.

Albert Leonard, Jr., Department of Art History and Archaeology, University of Missouri-Columbia.

Rebecca Mersereau, Department of Art History and Archaeology, University of Missouri-Columbia.

David Soren, Department of Art History and Archaeology, University of Missouri-Columbia.

CHRONOLOGICAL TABLE*

Neolithic, Khirokitia culture		7000–6000 B.C.
Neolithic, Sotira culture		4500–3750 B.C.
Chalcolithic	I	3500–2500/2300 B.C.
Early Bronze Age	I	2300–2075 B.C.
	II	2075–2000 B.C.
	III	2000–1900 B.C.
Middle Bronze Age	I	1900–1800 B.C.
	II	1800–1725 B.C.
	III	1725–1625 B.C.
Late Bronze Age	I	1625–1450 B.C.
	II	1450–1225 B.C.
	III	1225–1050 B.C.
Geometric	I	1050–950 B.C.
	II	950–850 B.C.
	III	850–750 B.C.
Archaic	I	750–600 B.C.
	II	600–475 B.C.
Classical	I	475–400 B.C.
	II	400–325 B.C.

*The absolute dates are approximate.

This chronology follows that proposed by V. Karageorghis, E.J. Peltenburg, and S. Swiny in Tatton-Brown, 1979.

Introduction

INTRODUCTION

Jane C. Biers
and
David Soren

Publication of these papers is the result of a symposium, "Recent Developments in Cypriote Archaeology," held at the University of Missouri-Columbia on October 13, 1979, to celebrate 25 years of involvement by the University of Missouri in the archaeology of Cyprus. As part of the celebration, an exhibition, "Art of Ancient Cyprus: Twenty-five Years of Missouri in Cyprus," opened in the Museum of Art and Archaeology on October 12, preceded by a lecture by the guest of honor, Dr. Vassos Karageorghis, Director of the Department of Antiquities on Cyprus. The occasion was marked by an opening address by Dr. Norma Kershaw, at the time president of the Cyprus American Archaeological Research Institute (CAARI) in Nicosia.

The University of Missouri has a longstanding connection with the archaeology of Cyprus. Several Cypriote objects now in the collection of the Museum of Art and Archaeology were the property of the University well before the Museum was founded in 1957. With the exception of a stone bowl from Khirokitia, the exact provenience and acquisition date of these objects are not known, but the Neolithic sherds probably also came from Khirokitia. The University is fortunate to possess these sherds since it is rare to find Neolithic material outside the museums of Cyprus and Sweden. Several fine vases dating to the Early Bronze Age are also part of this early acquisition.

In 1951, Saul S. Weinberg, Professor Emeritus of Archaeology and former director of the Museum of Art and Archaeology, began work on the architecture of the Late Bronze Age settlement at Bamboula, east of the village of Episkopi on the south coast of Cyprus. He had been invited to complete the publication left unfinished at the untimely death of John Franklin Daniel, who excavated the site for the University of Pennsylvania from 1937 to 1948. While in Cyprus working on this publication (Weinberg 1981), Professor Weinberg discovered the Bronze Age site of Phaneromeni, also near the village of Episkopi. In 1955 he returned to Cyprus with the Missouri-Cyprus Expedition, supported by funds from the Research Council of the University of Missouri. The excavations uncovered a Bronze Age cemetery; three tomb groups from the cemetery comprise the University's share of the finds. Professor Weinberg's work at Phaneromeni is being continued by Dr. James Carpenter of Kent State University, a Missouri alumnus, who began work in 1975. A report on his excavations is included here.

After the 1955 expedition, Missouri continued its interest in Cyprus. In 1959, the Museum acquired 39 objects from the Cyprus Museum, Nicosia, in exchange for books. Professor Paul Åström from the University of Göteborg, Sweden, spent the

year 1963 to 1964 at the University of Missouri-Columbia as visiting associate professor. His seminar on Cypriote archaeology formed the basis for the subsequent publication of the Cypriote collection of the Museum of Art and Archaeology (Åström, Biers,
and others, 1978).

The University's support of and interest in Cypriote archaeology resulted in
further acquisition of Cypriote objects for the Museum of Art and Archaeology.
Three Early Bronze Age tomb groups from the late James R. Stewart's excavations
for the University of Sydney, Australia, were acquired in 1973, two from Ayia
Paraskevi near Nicosia, and one from Lapatsa on the north coast.

The most recent ventures in Cyprus by the University of Missouri began in
1977 with the reopening of excavations at one of the famous sanctuaries of the
ancient world, that of Apollo Hylates at Kourion, also near Episkopi. Excavation
there by General Luigi Palma di Cesnola was begun in the 1870s, but the first
serious excavations were made between 1934 and 1952 by the University of Pennsylvania under the direction of George McFadden and Professor B.H. Hill. In 1977,
the Department of Antiquities turned over the site to David Soren, Associate
Professor of Art History and Archaeology at the University of Missouri-Columbia.
Soren and Dr. Diana Buitron of The Walters Art Gallery are, at present, co-directing
the project, which was the subject of a 25 minute color documentary film made by the
University of Missouri in the summer of 1980. That summer also saw increased involvement in Cyprus with a survey of the area around Episkopi conducted by Albert
Leonard, Jr., Associate Professor of Art History and Archaeology at the University
of Missouri-Columbia.

Thus, in the past 25 years Missouri has maintained a firm interest in the archaeology of Cyprus, an interest whose beginnings go back to an even earlier period.
The exhibition and the symposium commemorated those years of fruitful work. The
papers presented in this volume are a symbol of continued successful undertakings.

A paper presented at the symposium by Lawrence Stager, "The Excavations at
Idalion, Cyprus," was not available for publication. Two papers on topics relevant
to the current excavations at the Sanctuary of Apollo Hylates at Kourion have, therefore, been substituted, together with a third on the pottery from Kalavasos to supplement Rebecca Mersereau's excavation report, "The 1979 Vasilikos Valley Project."

The story of civilization on Cyprus begins, as far as is known, with the aceramic
Neolithic period when settlers came perhaps from the Syrian coast. Particular attention has been given to the impressive site of Khirokitia, first investigated in the
1930s. Here hillside dwellers built circular mud brick and stone buildings and perhaps traded with Anatolia and the Levant between ca. 7000 and 6000 B.C. Khirokitia
is today again the subject of intensive excavation. Dr. A. LeBrun of the French
Centre de la Recherche Scientifique has been working there since 1975.

The Khirokitia culture ended ca. 6000 B.C., followed by about 1500 years for
which little evidence of occupation has been found. The Sotira culture, named after
a site on a steep hill near the south coast, began ca. 4500 B.C. and shows no
connection with the earlier culture. The settlements, of which as many as 25 have
been recognized, were agricultural villages with single room, roughly oval houses
built on stone socles. The inhabitants of the southern settlements produced comb-
impressed pottery; those of the northern, pots with painted patterns. Otherwise,
the sites are remarkably similar. There is evidence of occasional deer herding and
gathering of grapes and olives.

The Neolithic period is, however, still far from being completely understood, and the work of Dr. Ian Todd, representing Brandeis University and the National Science Foundation, is significant. Todd's work in the Vasilikos valley just south of Khirokitia provided evidence of the aceramic Neolithic at Kalavasos-Tenta. Again, round houses are seen on a hill, now surrounded by a defensive wall and ditch. Todd found the first example of ancient painting on Cyprus, a human figure done in red ochre. He also unearthed evidence showing that the Neolithic architects at Tenta were rather more experimental than one would have expected. Todd's work is summarized in this publication, with permission, by Rebecca Mersereau, a graduate student at the University of Missouri and former student with the Brandeis team. A preliminary report by Dr. Susan Kromholz on the earlier prehistoric pottery from the Vasilikos valley also is included.

The Chalcolithic (literally copper-stone) period which followed the Neolithic, ca. 3500 B.C., is an obscure period, although recent advances in understanding it have been made. It seems to have lasted longer in the southern part of the island, as suggested by Dr. Ellen Herscher in this volume. Chalcolithic Cyprus is the special study of Dr. E.J. Peltenburg of the University of Edinburgh who, since 1975, has been excavating at Lemba Lakkous on the southwest coast near Paphos. Other settlements have been excavated near Erimi in the vicinity of Sotira. During the Chalcolithic metal began to be used, and the population seems to have expanded throughout the island. Cemeteries and elaborate grave goods were introduced, and attractive stone cruciform idols appear as a new type of figurine. The houses at Lemba are single room structures; Peltenburg has shown they had a specialized function, such as kitchen or workshop, rather than being solely living quarters.

The symposium reported on the curious Chalcolithic site at Ayious dug by Todd in 1978 as part of an emergency mission to beat the then rapidly progressing Larnaca-Limassol road. Among some 50 pits filled with unusual soil that moved slightly when pressed lightly with the fingers, Todd found several that look like chamber tombs with their tops missing, but are not. Are they perhaps 2 m. deep work areas with underground passages or simply shelters from the wind as the Vasilikos Valley Project's Alison South suggests after attempting to work there in the winter of 1980?

The really controversial period on Cyprus is the Bronze Age, represented in this publication by several important articles. Was this a time of rapidly expanding populations or depopulation? What kinds of pottery were being made? Where are the Early Bronze Age sites once thought so numerous on Cyprus? Every year at the meeting of the Cyprus American Archaeological Research Institute in Nicosia, scholars gather to debate these questions and present new evidence.

Much of the chronological dispute centers around the dating of pottery types: their evolution, decoration, and frequency. Red Polished ware was once thought to typify only the Early Bronze Age, but now, as Ellen Herscher shows, the problem is much more complex. Scholars are becoming increasingly aware of regionalism in Bronze Age Cyprus. Cultural development may lag in some parts of the island and rapidly advance in others. Early Cypriote may be lacking in the southwest, and Chalcolithic may linger on without the need to imagine a depopulation of the area. One is hampered also by a scarcity of Early and Middle Bronze Age settlements; numerous tombs have been excavated, but they can only tell a limited story.

Stewart Swiny, recent Ph.D. of the University of London and Director of CAARI, has made important surveys of Bronze Age sites in southern Cyprus and has evaluated regional settlement patterns. Dr. James Carpenter, working along with

Swiny and Herscher, has excavated the important site at Phaneromeni near Episkopi. Reevaluating Weinberg's earlier work at the site, they believe now that the main settlement was a small farming community dating from about 1600 B.C. which was dramatically destroyed by fire. Swiny believes that this is just one of many sites in this densely inhabited region which ended at the conclusion of the Late Cypriote IA period. The site of Phaneromeni does not seem to have been inhabited in the Early Bronze Age, but the matter is still open to dispute. The Phaneromeni publication presented here is the first major work by the current excavator about this site and so is of particular importance.

Alambra, between Nicosia and Khirokitia, is another important site recently investigated. Here, Dr. John Coleman of Cornell University has located domestic architecture of the early Middle Bronze Age. His unusual pottery distributions are important for understanding regionalism in this area and are being published by Jane Barlow.

The Late Bronze Age witnesses the coming of writing and a reduction of the earlier regionalism. In this period, an enormous number of wealthy sites produced fabulous art treasures, many of which are scattered today among the great museums of the Western world. The cause of all of this wealth was increased trade in copper, mined and smelted in a manner recently discovered by Dr. Frank Koucky. Near Eastern, Egyptian, and Mycenaean influences provided new objects for daily life and even effected religious changes.

Dr. Paul Åström has made spectacular discoveries at Hala Sultan Tekke, where previously very rich tombs had been found by the British. This early 12th century site yielded a stunning 86 cm.-long bronze trident worthy of Poseidon, as well as jewelry and other objects of lapis lazuli, gold, silver, faience, and ivory. Dr. Åström's knowledge of Bronze Age pottery remains an important source for scholars studying the pottery of this period, and his discussion with Jane Barlow of the chronological significance of the Alambra wares was a highlight of the 1979 CAARI meeting.

Roughly contemporary with Tekke is the heavily fortified site of Maa just north of Paphos, now being studied by Dr. Karageorghis who also conducted recent rescue work in tombs at Kouklia southeast of Palaeopaphos. These tombs range in date from the Late Bronze Age to the Hellenistic period. In one Mycenaean tomb of long dromos type, Karageorghis discovered a bronze spit with an 11th century inscription which is of great importance for determining possible Achaean origin of an early Cypriote dialect. A report on this excavation is included in this publication.

Also at Kouklia, a Swiss-German team under the direction of Dr. F. G. Maier recently uncovered Late Bronze Age architectural remains which show that the temple of Aphrodite was originally built ca. 1200 B.C. Previously, the temple was thought to be Roman.

At Kition near Larnaca, Karageorghis has unearthed an astonishing complex of large temples with sacred gardens which were at their peak after 1200 B.C. Copper smelting workshops just adjacent confirm the close relationship of religion to the chief economic basis of the island. Enkomi, too, allegedly founded by heroes of the Trojan War, blossomed in the 13th century and seems to have furnished an early example of orthogonal city planning. Similar gridding is appearing at Ian Todd's Late Cypriote II rescue operation at Ayios Dhimitrios.

The Geometric period normally signifies the coming of the Iron Age to a Mediterranean community, but Cypriote iron weapons already were known in the 12th century.

The period between 1050 and 850 B.C. is still obscure, but the discoveries at Kouklia are helping to elucidate the 9th century. At Kition, an important Phoenician community was established ca. 850, effecting profound changes in the area's pottery and life styles. Late in this period, the rise of Assyria became a major threat to the independent island.

Cyprus yielded in 709 B.C., and each of its kingdoms paid tribute until another force, Egypt, restored a balance of power to the eastern Mediterranean. Egyptian domination of Cyprus lasted but a few years in the middle of the 6th century, but cultural influences lasted longer. The sanctuary of Kourion, possibly founded before 600 B.C., has strong cult ties with the Near East, particularly with Canaanite religion, but other influences also were present. In her discussion of a bronze belt from the sanctuary, Hillary Browne, graduate student at Missouri and an area supervisor at the site, points out the hybrid character of Cypriote art from about 600 to 550 B.C. An archaic, cubical stamp-seal from the same site, published here by Missouri graduate student/site surveyor Michael Arwe, is yet another example of artistic eclecticism drawing on Syrian, Egyptian, Greek, and Phoenician work. This eclecticism is reflected in other sites as well, including Kition, Salamis, Amathus, and Idalion.

Kourion is an important site on the island because its cult goes back to the most remote periods of Cypriote life. Sacred andesite cone stones, known from seventh millennium Khirokitia, are the primitive ancestors of those found in 1979 at Kourion's Sanctuary of Apollo. The round cult building or Tholos, discovered in 1979, contained a sacred grove or garden area and was raised on an artificial high place, recalling Canaanite Bronze Age practices. Sacred trees are discussed by Darice Birge, a graduate student at the University of California, Berkeley, and an area supervisor at Kourion, while in another article Stephen Glover, a Missouri graduate student, describes the cult of Apollo on Cyprus and offers parallels for the Kourion baetyls and tree worship.

Following a period of Persian control, Cyprus alternated among Greek, Persian, Egyptian, and finally Roman domination. The latter influence is witnessed by the stunning mosaics of Nea Paphos and the buildings of Kourion and Salamis. New evidence indicates that the final destruction of southwest Cyprus was caused by a terrible series of earthquakes in 370 A.D. Not only Kourion, but Paphos, too, may have ended at this time.

The religious and cultural practices documented by scholars in this symposium have not died. Transformed by invasion, passage of time, and exposure to new ideas, the ancient practices can still be seen when one visits the sacred stone in the Sotira town square or the sacred tree of Ayia Solomoni. Through archaeology one learns to understand why a culture behaves today as it does and these symposium articles should serve as a good, basic introduction to the legacies of Cyprus.

Part I

Vasilikos Valley

CHAPTER 1.

THE 1979 VASILIKOS VALLEY PROJECT

Rebecca Mersereau

Approximately midway between modern Larnaca and Limassol, the Vasilikos valley stretches from its origins in the foothills of the Troodos Mountains down to the southern shore of Cyprus (Figure 1-1). The summer of 1979 was the fourth season for the Project in this valley, a valley which is proving to be one of the most bountiful areas on Cyprus for archaeological remains (Todd 1977a, 1977b, 1978; Todd et al. 1978, 1979a, and 1979b). With a staff of, at times, over 30 persons, Dr. Ian A. Todd, Director of the Project, supervised excavations in 1979 at Kalavasos-Tenta, a rescue excavation at Kalavasos-Ayious, and a field survey of the entire valley. Excavation was also begun at a third site discovered by C. Polycarpou in 1976. This site, located approximately 300 m. south/southwest of Tenta, is now called Kalavasos-Ayios Dhimitrios. The village of Kalavasos, lying 6 km. inland, was the excavation team's headquarters.

Tenta, about 2.5 km. south/southeast of Kalavasos, is an aceramic Neolithic settlement approximately contemporary with its better-known neighbor, Khirokitia (Karageorghis 1979: 686-689). One of the many goals of the Tenta excavations was to find transitional strata from the aceramic to the ceramic Neolithic, but all of the architecture so far exposed there dates to the aceramic period (ca. 5500 B.C.); the only remains of the later ceramic phase (ca. 3500 B.C.) are some pits with ceramic deposits. Because, however, the extant structures of the aceramic phase comprise many types and have been discovered in such a remarkable state of preservation, work will continue at this site.

The plan of Tenta (Figure 1-2) shows that all the structures excluding the piers are curvilinear. Some are built entirely of stone, others of mud brick on a stone foundation, and others purely of mud brick. In addition, there are two other types of construction: buildings with stone inner walls and mud brick outer walls, and the reverse, mud brick inner walls and outer stone reinforcing walls. Depending on the size of the structure, many have at least one, some two, internal piers, probably to support a second story. Interior walls and floors are usually plastered, and some floors have small areas of stone paving. All the larger structures are probably domestic, and one smaller structure seems designed for storage. In some areas, three construction phases are so far attested.

The significance of the Tenta architecture is that all these various building methods are found in approximately contemporary phases, showing that a great deal of trial and experimentation by the Neolithic inhabitants took place in a relatively short space of time. The extremely good state of preservation of these buildings, many to a height of 1 m., is also unusual.

An important discovery was made on the southern slope of the site in the 1979 season. It was in this lower area that Dr. Dikaios, former Director of the Department of Antiquities on Cyprus, first dug in 1947 (Dikaios 1960: pl. 18; Todd 1977a: 12-13). He exposed part of a thick outer wall. Some evidence for the existence of a ditch outside this wall was found in 1978. Further excavation was accomplished here in 1979 with the result that more domestic structures, several burials, and, most importantly, a deep ditch were revealed. The bottom of the ditch was reached at the west end of the excavation area. The bottom surface was rather irregular; at some time, it had been filled in with large stones. The purpose of this broad wall and its ditch is not clear, although it may be presumed to be of a defensive nature.

A major find at Tenta in the 1979 season was a red ochre human figure painted on the east face of the internal pier of structure 11 (Figure 1-3). The figure is about 40 cm. high, rather crudely drawn, with a square head, upraised arms, and elongated neck. The painted plaster was not in a good state of preservation, and it seems likely that originally there was at least one other figure. After testing different conservation methods, a consolidant was applied, and the southern section of the painting was removed, while the northern section remains in situ. This is the only Neolithic wall painting on Cyprus and, therefore, is of great significance (Todd: in press).

Five more burials were found at Tenta in 1979, bringing the total to ten. They were placed both within and outside structures; none were found with accompanying grave goods.

Approximately 500 m. due east of Tenta, across the river valley, a plateau rises on which lies the site of Kalavasos-Ayious. Ayious, besides being a later, ceramic Chalcolithic site, is of a completely different nature from Tenta. At Ayious there is no extant standing architecture. A cluster of approximately 50 pits of various shapes and sizes has been excavated. Some pits are as large as 2.75 m. in diameter and 2 m. deep (Figure 1-4). In many of the larger pits, lumps of daub, presumably the remains of a collapsed superstructure, were found, while some of the smaller pits were plainly hearths or ovens. The complex of pits and subterranean tunnels discovered at the northern end of the site is exceptional. Although the fill of this complex and most of the larger pits at Ayious was of a domestic nature, Dr. Todd hesitates to designate these pits as dwellings and hopes that further artifactual analyses will provide the evidence needed to understand the site as a whole. As mentioned previously, Ayious is a rescue excavation because of the planned route of the new Nicosia-Limassol highway which will destroy the central area of the site.

The third site, Ayios Dhimitrios, is located approximately 300 m. south/southwest of Tenta. It can now be described with certainty as being a Late Bronze Age town of major importance. Because of the impending construction of the highway which will pass through the very center of the site, an extensive rescue operation was mounted.

In general, excavation was restricted to uncovering the tops of walls, and only a few soundings penetrated to further depths (Figure 1-5). Early findings included rectilinear architecture, large ceramic storage jars, and Late Cypriote II pottery. The architectural construction was of fine quality, and two architectural phases have been ascertained with some re-use of ashlar blocks. Above all, the architecture exhibits a high degree of planning and organization, perhaps even to the extent that a grid plan may have been implemented here as at Enkomi.

The intended function of many structures and features in the eastern portion of the site remains unclear. Features found in it include a large ceramic bath, and, in another area, a deliberately sloping floor for liquid to flow down into a sunken pithos. A well with pottery and deer and cattle bones in its lowest levels was also found. The area excavated so far does not appear to be purely domestic, but it cannot yet be determined if specialized activities were undertaken in different areas of the site.

Roughly 150 m. to the west of the eastern area more stone walls on nearly the same alignment were revealed. Between the eastern and western areas four chamber tombs were uncovered, and even though disturbed in antiquity, two of them still contained a good deal of pottery, human skeletal material, a few metal objects, and some decorated ivory pieces. The pottery shows that Tomb 1 is of the same date as the settlement, Late Cypriote II C, but the ceramics in Tomb 4 date it to Late Cypriote I or early Late Cypriote II.

The discoveries at Ayios Dhimitrios mark it as one of the Late Bronze Age centers on Cyprus. Its prosperity and importance may be linked to copper mining, for the town now called Ayios Dhimitrios was very strategically located, both for control of the copper mines that lie north of Kalavasos and for control of the primary east-west route along the southern coast of the island.

One of the goals of the Vasilikos Valley Project is to complete a field survey of the entire valley. All sites from prehistoric through medieval are being recorded in order to compile data on the settlement system of the valley. At this time, 58 sites have been located.

The Vasilikos Valley Project has taken a multidisciplinary approach to the study of the valley as a whole. All data relevant to the valley's environmental and economic systems are being recorded so that the life in the valley in earlier times may be reconstructed and seen in its broader milieu.

ACKNOWLEDGMENTS

This material is based upon work supported by the National Science Foundation under Grant no. BNS77-07685 AO2.

I would like to thank Dr. Ian A. Todd, Director of the Vasilikos Valley

Project, for generously giving me permission to present a paper on the 1979 season and to publish it here. This report has been updated since its presentation in October of 1979 with additional information kindly supplied by Dr. Todd.

1-3. Kalavasos-Tenta: Drawing of the southern section of the wall painting on the east face of the pier within Structure 11. Drawn by A. South.

1-4. Kalavasos-Ayious: Pit 1 in square C 11 C, from the southeast. Photograph by I.A. Todd.

1-5. Kalavasos-Ayios Dhimitrios: General view of the east area within the line of the new road, from the west. Photograph by A. South.

CHAPTER 2

A PRELIMINARY REPORT ON THE EARLIER PREHISTORIC

CERAMICS OF THE VASILIKOS VALLEY

Susan Kromholz

INTRODUCTION*

The Vasilikos Valley Project is a multidisciplinary archaeological project designed
to study the entire Vasilikos river valley system in the Larnaca District of southern
Cyprus (Todd 1977a, 1977b, 1978; Todd et al. 1978, 1979a, 1979b; Mersereau, this
volume). One research goal is to clarify the pottery sequence in this south coastal
region of Cyprus from the Neolithic through the Bronze Age. While specific evidence
concerning the transition from the aceramic to the ceramic Neolithic has yet to be
found, considerably more than 100,000 sherds that might be assigned to the Late
Neolithic and Chalcolithic periods have been collected in four seasons of field work.
Of these sherds, less than a third are derived from excavated contexts. The re-
mainder were obtained by surface collection during the field survey of the valley.
Forty-thousand sherds have been studied to date,[1] the majority of which are derived
from three sites lying close together adjacent to the Vasilikos river. The ceramic
material from these sites provides a relative sequence probably dating to the Chalcolithic period.

The term Chalcolithic has, in the past, been rather loosely employed in Cypriote
archaeology. Generally (following the scheme of periods outlined by Dikaios 1962:
177 ff), it has been applied to several sites and assemblages whose main common
element is thin-line Red-on-White painted pottery,[2] first identified by Dikaios at
the Chalcolithic type-site of Erimi-Pamboules (Dikaios 1936). Unfortunately, prehistoric Cypriotes, unlike their mainland counterparts, seldom occupied a settlement
site for more than one cultural phase, and Chalcolithic pottery has not been found in
a multi-period stratified context. Attempts have been made to trace the development
of Chalcolithic ceramics within a single site (Dikaios' work at Erimi is the classic
study), but comparisons among sites have not, in the past, been useful in establishing
a developmental sequence for the Chalcolithic period. Although Peltenburg (1979:9)
suggests that the Erimi features found at Lapithos and Kythrea are sufficient to

* This paper was submitted for publication while Dr. Kromholz was in Korea. As
director of the Vasilikos Valley Project, I assumed the task of editing it in her absence
and am responsible for any errors which may have arisen in this process. Ian A. Todd

17

call those sites part of a general Erimi culture, he also emphasizes the lack of archaeological data available and writes that the Lemba Project (of which he is the director) "was initiated to deal with some of what are judged to be the most outstanding
problems" of the Chalcolithic period (ibid.: 11).

What has been needed for a meaningful study of Chalcolithic ceramics is a
series of closely related but discrete sites, all of which might be assigned (at least
in part) to the Chalcolithic, but which do not have identical ceramic assemblages.
Peltenburg (ibid.: 35ff) identified such a series (Lemba-Lakkous, Kissonerga-
Mosphilia, and Kissonerga-Mylouthkia) in the Paphos region; another has been discovered in the Vasilikos valley.

The three Vasilikos valley sites lie within 2 km. of one another near the Vasilikos
river. Besides their close geographical proximity, the sites--Kalavasos-Tenta,
Kalavasos-Ayious, and Kalavasos-Kokkinoyia/Pamboules--share a set of distinctive
ceramic characteristics which suggest a cultural link and may represent a sequence
of Chalcolithic period occupation. Although all the ceramic material from the sites
has not yet been studied, preliminary evidence suggests that several stylistic and
constructional factors which have been isolated can serve as chronological markers
for the individual sites.

KALAVASOS-TENTA

Introduction

Kalavasos-Tenta is essentially an aceramic Neolithic settlement site (Mersereau,
this volume). Ceramics were collected from the lower flanks of the western and
southern sides of the site during the initial survey (Todd et al. 1978: 170), but
subsequent excavation in the northwest sector (grid square B 7 C) did not yield
pottery in a stratified context (Todd et al. 1979a: 16, 18). Ceramics also were found
on the surface near the northeast edge of the site (square K 7) (Todd et al. 1979a:
18; 1979b: 276-277). Excavation there revealed a truncated pit containing three
possible floors, with some ceramics found in association with each floor (Paul Croft,
personal communication).

The largest group of sherds excavated at Tenta, however, was obtained from a
deep depression visible in the eroded east section of the site. During the 1978 excavation season, a sounding was made there in square O 16 B in the hope that it
would provided stratified ceramic remains. Unfortunately, the sherds seem to be in
a secondary context, washed down into the depression from the higher parts of the
site, and the stratigraphy of the area is problematical (Todd et al. 1979a: 18; 1979b:
276). For this reason, the ceramics from O 16 B are considered as a single unit without reference to the individual levels recognized in the sounding.

Perhaps the most striking feature of the Tenta pottery, aside from its poor con-
dition due to heavy incrustation (Kromholz 1979: 35-36), is the overwhelming presence of a distinctive light-colored fabric. This fabric (called Fabric A) is white or

buff (10YR 8/2, 8/3, 7/3; 2.5Y 8/2, 7/2, 7/4)[3] and has been completely oxidized during firing. It is homogeneous and very hard, with grit inclusions. Small numbers of fine ware sherds are of a totally different fabric (called Fabric B). Sandy in texture and laminated, this fabric varies in exterior surface color from orange (2.5YR 5/6; 5YR 5/5, 5/6, 6/6) to brown (5YR 5/3; 7.5YR 5/4, 7/6). Fabric B is usually not fully oxidized; it contains both inorganic and organic inclusions of varying sizes. The latter are most common near the interior surfaces of closed vessels. Of the fine ware sherds found in 0 16 B, 85 percent belong to Fabric A and 15 percent to Fabric B.

Coarse ware at Tenta consists of a soft fabric with large inorganic inclusions in addition to many organic inclusions. In color, the fabric ranges from red to black (2.5YR 3.5/5-4/5, 2.5/0; 5YR 4.5/4; 7.5YR 5/3, 4/2; 10YR 3/2).

Ware Types [4]

Six separate types have been identified at Tenta. The fine wares include Combed, Painted-and-Combed, Red-on-White, and Monochrome wares. This last category is a catchall applied to undecorated sherds regardless of color. When dealing with the Vasilikos valley ceramics, it is impossible to ascertain from a single undecorated sherd whether it belonged to a decorated or undecorated vessel. Fabric, color, and surface treatment are identical for all the fine wares. Further, firing is irregular, resulting in mottled vessels with red, orange, and black areas (10YR 4/4, 5/7; 2.5YR 4/3-5/8; 5YR 5.5/5-5.5/6; 10YR 4.5/1, 3/1, 3/2). The coarse wares include Coarse and Dark Burnished, which is, in fabric, a coarser version of Fabric B resembling the darker coarse ware vessels in color (5YR 5/1, 5/3; 7.5YR 5/3).[5]

Surface Treatment

At Tenta, Monochrome, Combed, Dark Burnished, and Coarse ware vessels appear to have been slipped. On Dark Burnished and Coarse ware vessels, a self-slip seems to have been used; but this observation is the result of superficial, non microscopic examination. Monochrome and Combed ware vessels are covered with a rather thick, even slip that fires both red and black.

Painted-and-Combed and Red-on-White ware vessels are not slipped. The painted pattern is applied directly to the smoothed surface of the vessel; the paint seems to be of the same consistency and color as the slip used on the Monochrome and Combed ware vessels. It is not surprising that many Red-on-White ware vessels at Tenta are made of Fabric A, since this fabric's light surface provides a contrast to the darker paint.

All vessels, regardless of ware, display clear evidence of smoothing and burnishing. Coarse and Dark Burnished ware vessels are burnished comparatively unevenly (although some Dark Burnished ware sherds do have a very extensively burnished surface) with wide, deep grooves resulting. The fine wares are more evenly burnished, although the quality ranges from relatively careless overlapping strokes to beautifully smooth surfaces.

Shapes

Vessels found at Tenta include both open and closed shapes. In the fine wares, deep and shallow bowls occur (Figure 2-1: 1-16, 19) with round and omphalos bases. Closed vessels include jugs and jars with round horizontal mouths and cylindrical necks (Figure 2-2: 1-3) and a number of different base configurations, such as round, flat, and omphalos. Peg bases are found at Tenta, but not in square 0 16 B. Dark Burnished ware shapes include deep, straight-sided bowls (Figure 2-2: 4-5, 7) and holemouth vessels (Figure 2-2: 6) with heavy lug handles (Figure 2-2: 7-8). Coarse ware vessels include bowls (Figure 2-2: 10, 14-15), holemouth vessels (Figure 2-2: 11), and jars (Figure 2-2: 9). The most common shape, however, is the flat-bottomed shallow tray with a flanged base. One complete profile has been found (Figure 2-2: 16). These trays range from vessels with rather thin walls to considerably cruder vessels (Figure 2-2:13). Some of the trays lack the flange, and two rare sherds show evidence of a drain (?) hole above the base (Figure 2-2: 12).[6] There is no evidence of basket impressions on the bottoms of the trays.

Construction Techniques

The construction technique used by the Tenta potters was the same for all vessel shapes and wares. This technique, involving the addition of multiple layers to the surfaces of an inner or core vessel, is unusual, and seems to provide a chronological marker for the study of ceramics in the Vasilikos valley.

Tenta vessels are coil built. After the coiled vessel had partially dried, the potter applied layers of clay to the outer surface of closed vessels, and to both the outer and inner surfaces of open vessels. Evidence suggests that these layers were paddled on to the coiled core-vessels proceeding from the base to the rim ("paddle and anvil" technique). This hypothesis, however, has not yet been tested by practical experimentation. As a result of the two-fold construction process, this pottery tends to break apart while buried in the ground. Typically, the surface layers separate from the inner vessel, probably as a result of the action of ground water.

Some of the closed vessels appear to have been constructed over a woven reed form. Impressions found on the interior of jug fragments (and identified earlier (Kromholz 1979: 39) as possibly representing an anvil utilized in the paddling process) are now believed to have been left by a reed framework. Some neck sherds from closed vessels also show evidence of having been formed using a stick or reed tool as a support for the inner surface.

Decoration

The combed, painted-and-combed, and painted patterns found at Tenta are not unusual for Late Neolithic/Early Chalcolithic pottery in Cyprus. Patterns on Combed ware sherds include vertical, horizontal, and diagonal bands of straight and rippled parallel lines (Figure 2-3: 1-3). A rare pattern (found on only one sherd) consists of a series of overlapping diagonal bands (Figure 2-3: 2).

The combing on the Painted-and-Combed ware sherds is generally confined to vertical or diagonal painted bands (Figure 2-3: 4-6), but some vessels are decorated with triangular painted patterns filled with combed lines (Figure 2-3: 9-11). Rarely, these are found in conjunction with painted lattice patterns (Figure 2-3: 10). Horizontal combing is also found (Figure 2-3: 7-8), but is far less common than vertical combing.

There seems to be no standardization in the tools used to create the combed patterns. Some artists utilized tools with beautifully even and finely cut teeth (Figure 2-3: 4, 7, 8, 11), while others used cruder and more irregular tools (Figure 2-3: 1, 3, 6).

The painted patterns found on the Red-on-White ware are similarly simple, consisting for the most part of parallel lines. Vertical (Figure 2-4: 3, 5, 6, 13), horizontal (Figure 2-4: 3, 9, 10, 13) and diagonal (Figure 2-4: 1, 2, 4, 7) lines flank broad expanses of white or red. In some cases, already defined areas are filled with parallel lines (Figure 2-4: 10). Generally, the lines are carefully painted, and an attempt to keep the thickness constant is apparent. Occasionally, a painter used lines of widely differing widths to create his pattern (Figure 2-4: 1, 13).

Bowl rims are often decorated with a broad or narrow horizontal band (Figure 2-4: 1, 3-5), but this is not always the case (Figure 2-4: 2-4, 6). The presence or absence of this horizontal line on the rim does not seem to be correlated with the other patterns appearing on either face of the vessel. At Tenta, no constant correlations among patterns, or between pattern and vessel shape, have been noted. Except for the previously mentioned horizontal line on the rim of bowls and the frequent application of a band of horizontal parallel lines to the neck-shoulder join on closed vessels (Figure 2-4: 9a-b), no set decorative format is apparent at Tenta.

Finally, a few examples of a checkerboard pattern were found at Tenta (Figure 2-4: 11), and one fragmentary sherd may have been painted with concentric circles (Figure 2-4: 12). Simple as the patterns are, however, they are carefully executed and indicate a high level of craftsmanship.

KALAVASOS-AYIOUS

Introduction

The Chalcolithic site of Kalavasos-Ayious lies on a plateau on the eastern edge of the Vasilikos valley approximately 500 m. east of Tenta (Todd et al. 1979a: 25 ff; 1979b: 278 ff; Mersereau, this volume). Before rescue excavation was undertaken in 1978, a complete surface collection was made on the site. More ceramic material (including several complete or almost complete vessels) was found during the 1978 and 1979 excavations at Ayious. Although slight differences exist between the material derived from surface collection and the excavated ceramics, the Ayious pottery may be considered as a single unit. For the purposes of this paper, sherds collected within 30 m. of the western edge of the plateau and from the eroded slope below it (where the highest concentration of prehistoric material was found), and the ceramics excavated in square C 11 C, which lies in the center line of the new road close to the edge of the plateau, are grouped together.[7]

Both Fabric A and Fabric B are present at Ayious and are identical to the Tenta Fabric A and Fabric B. As at Tenta, Fabric A is more common, comprising 69 percent of all fine ware sherds.

Ware Types

Six types have been identified at Ayious: Combed, Painted-and-Combed, Mono-chrome, Red-on-White, Dark Burnished, and Coarse ware. Combed, Painted-and-Combed, and Dark Burnished wares occur only rarely.

Surface Treatment

In general, the color and surface treatment of the Ayious ceramics are the same as at Tenta, although burnishing has frequently resulted in slightly more lustrous surfaces. The surfaces of the vessels are slightly harder at Ayious than at Tenta. Painted decoration is usually applied to the smoothed but unslipped surface of the vessel. In a few cases, however, a light-colored slip seems to have been employed; this light-colored slip is never found at Tenta.

Another difference between the Tenta and the Ayious ceramics is the application at Ayious of colored slips to certain coarse ware vessels. Deep, straight-sided bowls are often slipped with a buff matt slip (10YR 8/3: 7.5YR 7/4). Flat-bottomed trays are covered with a roughly burnished red slip (2.5YR 4.5/6; 5YR 4/6).

Shapes

The range of vessel shapes at Ayious is wider than at Tenta. Fine ware bowl rims, for example, include several configurations not present at Tenta (Figure 2-5: 1-16). Bowl bases found at Ayious are flat or omphalos in shape (Figure 2-5: 17, 18, 20, 21). Among the open-shape sherds is a single fragment of a saucer-shaped vessel with a flat base and convex interior (Figure 2-5:19).[8] Fine ware closed shapes include a rather wide range of rim and neck configurations (Figure 2-6: 1-6, 8-10; Figure 2-7: 1). Peg bases are the most common shape (Figure 2-6:11-13), although a few flat bases have been found (Figure 2-6:7). Tubular spouts, both horizontal and rising, are present in small numbers at Ayious (Figure 2-6: 14, 15), and an open "trough" spout (not seen by the author) has been reported (personal communication from Alice Kingsnorth).

The corpus of Coarse ware shapes at Ayious is the most varied and interesting from the site. Not only are the flanged base trays common at Tenta found at Ayious (Figure 2-8: 18-20), but also flat-bottomed trays without flanged bases (Figure 2-8: 16, 17); deep vessels with vertical sides and slight flanges at the base and lug handles (Figure 2-8: 8, 9, 13; Figure 2-9: 1-3); deep and shallow bowls with flaring sides (Figure 2-8: 1-4, 6, 7); holemouth vessels with lug handles, one with a string-hole beneath the rim (Figure 2-8: 10-12); and a tiny cup, the base of which is un-fortunately missing (Figure 2-8: 5). Also found at Ayious are several flat trays with very thin bases and low rounded sides (Figure 2-8: 14, 15) that seem to be restricted to this site in the Vasilikos valley.

Construction Techniques

At Ayious, potters constructed vessels using wide, flattened coils. The coils were overlapped, either on the outside or the inside, as construction of the vessel progressed (Figure 2-10: 1, 2). There is no evidence that the coils were pinched or smoothed together except in a superficial fashion. Ayious vessels tend to break apart along the lines of these coils, and the lack of pinching and smoothing is then clearly visible.

The evidence suggests that the potters paused several times during the coiling process and smoothed or paddled layers over both the interior and exterior of the vessel. Each new surface layer was smoothed over the edges of the previous layer, resulting at some points in as many as six separate layers. The joins between surface layers can be seen clearly on the interiors of closed vessels.

In some cases, closed vessels seem to have had a finishing layer of finely levigated clay added to the interior of the base. Base exteriors, especially in the case of peg bases, are finished with as many as four thick surface layers.

Necks were applied separately at Ayious, and were sometimes scraped vertically on the inside with reeds or small sticks, probably in an attempt to strengthen the join. Some vessels may have been constructed over woven reed forms. Unlike those from Tenta, Coarse ware flat-bottomed trays at Ayious bear clear basket impressions.

Decoration

The Combed ware and Painted-and-Combed ware, derived solely from the surface survey of the site, are fragmentary and rare. From the available evidence, it appears that Ayious combed and painted-and-combed patterns are rather simple, consisting of vertical or horizontal bands of parallel rippled lines. One Painted-and-Combed sherd shows a horizontal band of paint encircling a closed vessel at the neck-shoulder join, with a vertical band of paint, combed vertically, pendant from the horizontal band. This is the most complete combed pattern found at Ayious.

The red-on-white painted patterns at Ayious are varied. The majority of them include parallel lines. Vertical (Figure 2-11:5,8; Figure 2-12:10), horizontal, and diagonal (Figure 2-12:7) lines flank broad expanses of white or red, or wide painted bands (Figure 2-12:1, 17). Often the areas defined by the lines are triangular (Figure 2-11:10, 12, 13, 15; Figure 2-12:5, 8; Figure 2-7:2). Sometimes the lines are thick (Figure 2-11: 1, 2, 4, 9; Figure 2-12: 1, 6), and often a broad band of paint defines the neck-shoulder join of a closed vessel (Figure 2-11: 11) or the rim of an open vessel (Figure 2-11: 1, 2; Figure 2-7: 1). Shoulder-neck joins also are defined by parallel horizontal lines (Figure 2-11: 8, 10, 11; Figure 2-7: 2). On some vessels, areas defined by thicker lines are filled in by parallel straight lines (Figure 2-12: 4, 14), zigzag lines (Figure 2-11: 6; Figure 2-12: 12), or overlapping chevrons (Figure 2-11: 7; Figure 2-7: 1). Checkerboard patterns exist, always in association with parallel lines (Figure 2-11: 1; Figure 2-12: 2, 3, 6). When lines and bands intersect, the paint is allowed to run beyond the boundaries of the various areas (Figure 2-11: 5; Figure 2-12: 2, 3, 9), and intersecting bands of parallel lines are usually carelessly painted (Figure 2-12: 9, 10). Line widths vary considerably, and the impression given by the patterns is one of an artistic tradition not interested in precision. This impression is strengthened by the presence of one sherd painted with what can only be called blobs of thin red paint (Figure 2-11:3).

A few sherds are, however, precisely decorated. On some the parallel lines are evenly painted (Figure 2-11: 11, 12). One sherd has a zigzag line in reserve which is carefully executed (Figure 2-12: 13), as is the column of single dots on another sherd (Figure 2-12: 16). Several sherds have boldly painted wavy and zigzag lines in conjunction with carefully executed parallel vertical lines

(Figure 2-12: 14, 15, 17). Finally, two partially reconstructed vessels (one a holemouth vessel and the other a jug/jar) were very carefully decorated. The holemouth vessel (Figure 2-7: 1), which has at least three sets of paired string-holes spaced around the rim, is decorated with a broad band of paint at the rim. A series of broad vertical painted bands divides the vessel into an estimated five equal areas. Each area is filled with overlapping chevrons. The workmanship is careful, and the effect pleasing. The jug/jar (Figure 2-7: 2) is decorated with the most complex and also the most complete pattern found at Ayious. The neck-shoulder join is articulated by parallel horizontal lines. The body of the vessel is divided by unpainted vertical bands into several unequal areas, each containing a different motif. Four such areas can be seen on the reconstructed vessel, three of which are complete enough for the central motif (in each case shown in reserve) to be described. One area contains a large cross-shaped pattern, another, a band of three diagonal lines intersecting a band of three vertical lines, and the third, two narrow vertical bands flanking a wide vertical band.

KALAVASOS-KOKKINOYIA/PAMBOULES

Introduction

Kalavasos-Kokkinoyia/Pamboules is a complex of sites on a long ridge approximately 600 m. southeast of Ayious. The area includes Dikaios' sites of Kalavasos "A" and Kalavasos "B."[9] The site is being surveyed as part of the Vasilikos Valley Project, but as yet not all areas have been examined. A considerable number of sherds have been collected from Kalavasos-Kokkinoyia/Pamboules, and half of the material has not yet been processed. In Table 2-1, ceramic percentages are given for two surveyed plots (Cadastral Plan LV, Sheet 20, Plot 438 [divided into areas 1, 2, 3 NW, 3 NE, and 4 SW] and Plot 439 [NE, NW, SW]). Although these figures are derived from only one sector of the site, they are representative of all pottery processed thus far.

Both Fabric A and Fabric B are found at Kalavasos-Kokkinoyia/Pamboules. Fabric A seems to be identical with that found at Tenta and Ayious, but it is rare at Kokkinoyia/Pamboules, representing only 14 percent of the fine ware sherds. Fabric B at Kokkinoyia/Pamboules is more varied than at the other two sites, ranging from a fine paste with many small, inorganic inclusions to a heavily laminated fabric with large inorganic and many organic inclusions. Further work on the ceramics from the site would probably result in the division of the Kokkinoyia/Pamboules Fabric B into a series of fabric types.

The most intriguing aspect of the Kokkinoyia/Pamboules Fabric B is that, although the laminated variety appears to be homogeneous within any particular sherd, a distinctive pattern of differentially colored layers resulted from firing. No sherd found has fewer than two of these layers, and some have several. In the case of closed vessels, the following layering has been found: red/grey (2.5YR 4.5/6, 10 YR 4/2), orange/grey (5YR 5/6, 10YR 4/1), buff/grey (7.5YR 7.5/7, 10YR 6/2), and green/dark grey (5Y 5/3, 5Y 3/1), as well as orange/light orange (5YR 6/6, 10YR 6/4) and orange/red (2.5YR 5/6, 10R 5/8). One sherd, which was probably derived from the lower part of a large open vessel, has seven distinct layers (beginning from the exterior face of the vessel): orange (2.5YR 5/6), light orange (10YR 6/5), dark brown (10YR 3/1), brown (10YR 4/3), purple (10R 4/3), pink (10R 6/4), and red (2.5 YR 4.5/6). It is hoped that future testing and experimentation will help to explain this phenomenon which occurs in both Red-on-White and Monochrome ware sherds. At present, it seems that this color layering resulted from differential firing.

Ware Types

Five types have been found at Kalavasos-Kokkinoyia/Pamboules: Red-on-White, Monochrome, Coarse, Combed, and Painted-and-Combed wares. The latter two types are extremely rare in the material processed thus far.

Surface Treatment

Red-on-White ware at Kokkinoyia/Pamboules resembles, but is not identical to, that found at Tenta and Ayious. Unlike the ceramics from those sites, all vessels at Kokkinoyia/Pamboules appear to have been slipped. All fine wares, regardless of the final surface treatment, have been slipped with a chalky white slip (7.5YR 7.5/3; 10YR 7.5/2, 7.5/3, 8/3, 8/4; 2.5Y 8/2). The paint used on Red-on-White vessels is usually a rather bright red or deep orange (2.5YR 4.5/6-3/6, 5/6-5/7, 6/6; 5YR 3/2, 4/5-4/6, 5.5/4). Monochrome ware sherds range in color from red (10R 4/4, 5/7; 2.5YR 4/3-5/8; 5YR 5/5-5/6) to brown (5YR 4/3; 7.5YR 4.5/2) and black (2.5YR 3.5/0; 7.5YR 4/0; 10YR 3/1-4.5/1).

Coarse ware vessels at Kokkinoyia/Pamboules have either orange (2.5YR 3/6) or black (7.5YR 2/0) fabric and are slipped with a matt red slip (2.5YR 4/4-6/6). Unlike the coarse wares at Tenta and Ayious, those at Kokkinoyia/Pamboules are not burnished. Fine wares at the site are burnished, but the workmanship is not as careful as that seen at the other sites.

Shapes

The vessel shapes at Kokkinoyia/Pamboules are not substantially different from those described and illustrated by Dikaios (1962: 109 fig. 53; 137 fig. 64) for Kalavasos "A" and "B." Fine wares include bowls with straight and flaring sides (Figure 2-13 : 1-20), jugs with horizontal mouths (Figure 2-14: 1-5, 8), and hole-mouth vessels (Figure 2-14: 6, 7). Base shapes include peg (Figure 2-14; 9), omphalos (Figure 2-14; 10-11), pedestal (Figure 2-14: 12), and flat (Figure 2-14: 13-14). Rising tubular spouts are present but rare (Figure 2-14: 15), and no open spouts of the kind illustrated by Dikaios have been found. Lug handles are common (Figure 2-14: 16), the majority being unpierced.

Coarse ware is relatively uncommon at Kalavasos-Kokkinoyia/Pamboules. Several lug handles, both pierced (Figure 2-14: 19) and unpierced (Figure 2-14: 17, 18, 20), have been found. The most common Coarse ware shape, however, is the flat-bottomed tray which does not have a basket-impressed base. These trays sometimes have a flanged base (Figure 2-14: 21-23) and sometimes do not (Figure 2-14: 24), and the thickness of the walls and bases varies greatly. One example (Figure 2-14: 21) has a large drain (?) hole above the base[6]. Finally, among the Coarse ware sherds is one fragment of what might have been a heavy, saucer-shaped vessel (Figure 2-14: 25).

Construction Techniques

The ceramics of Kokkinoyia/Pamboules were constructed using the coil technique. Large vessels appear to have been made in two or more sections. Necks and spouts were made separately and joined to the body of the vessel after it had partially dried. There is no evidence for the addition of surface layers.

Decoration

The painted patterns at Kalavasos-Kokkinoyia/Pamboules are more complex than those found at Tenta or Ayious. Many of the basic elements are, however, similar: vertical parallel lines (Figure 2-15: 9, 18-20), horizontal parallel lines (Figure 2-15: 1, 8, 16), diagonal parallel lines (Figure 2-15: 3, 16-18), and checkerboard patterns (Figure 2-15: 1). In some cases, pattern-shape associations at Kokkinoyia/Pamboules are similar to those at Tenta and Ayious. A horizontal band along the rim of open vessels is an example of such an association (Figure 2-15: 1-4). The major decorative element at Kokkinoyia/Pamboules, however, is the lattice pattern. Lattice patterns, usually painted as a series of fairly even thin lines (Figure 2-15: 2), but sometimes utilizing lines of greatly differing widths (Figure 2-15: 15), fill areas of several shapes and sizes. Sometimes the lattice seems to be used alone to define roughly triangular areas of a vessel, and the strokes of the vertical lines are allowed to extend beyond the horizontal lines, creating a jagged edge (Figure 2-15: 6, 7, 11, 13). Occasionally, the horizontal lines in a lattice pattern are extended (Figure 2-15: 15). It seems likely that the rather common pattern of a series of short strokes generally found along the lower edge of a horizontal pattern (Figure 2-15: 4), but sometimes along the upper edge (Figure 2-15: 8, 16), is a development of the extended lattice pattern.

Lattice patterns are sometimes used to fill areas defined by straight lines. These lines may be thin (Figure 2-15: 11, 12) or thick (Figure 2-15: 5, 14, 17). When the defined areas are triangular or trapezoidal and rather small, the lowest corner is often finished with an extension of the vertical and horizontal outer lines (Figure 2-15: 5, 14). It seems likely that this, too, is a development of the extended lattice pattern, which is even further refined into a rare pattern of pairs of small right-angled strokes applied to the sides of other patterns (Figure 2-15: 10).

Dots as a decorative element are common at Kokkinoyia/Pamboules. Sometimes they are used to fill small triangular areas (Figure 2-15: 3), but more often they are found between parallel vertical lines. On some sherds dots are well painted and carefully spaced (Figure 2-15: 19), and on one unique sherd dots form a modified checkerboard pattern (Figure 2-15: 9). Occasionally, the dots are not carefully painted, and the resultant effect is one of horror vacui (Figure 2-15: 20).

COMPARISON OF THE CERAMICS FROM THE VASILIKOS VALLEY SITES

A comparison of the ceramics from the sites of Tenta, Ayious, and Kokkinoyia/Pamboules in the Kalavasos area seems to indicate that the three sites may be arranged in a chronological sequence, with the earliest material being found at Tenta and the latest at Kokkinoyia/Pamboules.[10] Several factors may be cited to support this sequence, of which the most obvious are also the most traditional: the stylistic features of ware types, surface treatment, vessel shapes, and decorative schemes. The use of Fabric A and the layered construction method are additional factors to be considered.

Ware Types

In the traditional typologies of Cypriote pottery, Combed, Painted-and-Combed, Dark Burnished, and the bold variety of Red-on-White wares are considered indicative of Neolithic period occupation; thin-line Red-on-White ware, of Chalcolithic date. Therefore, the presence or absence of these wares and their relative frequency of occurrence should provide some indication of the period of the site.

The question of identifying Red-on-White sherds as bold or thin-line is considered below; the frequency of occurrence of the other ware types mentioned previously is discussed here. Despite the fragmentary nature of the material under study, and the obvious biases present in the collection of surface material as compared with that derived from excavation and the small percentages involved, the amount of Combed, Painted-and-Combed and Dark Burnished wares decreases when the Tenta figures are compared with those of Ayious, and those of Ayious with Kokkinoyia/Pamboules. Of the sherds studied from Tenta, 1.4 percent are Combed ware, 0.6 percent are Painted-and-Combed ware, and 1 percent are Dark Burnished ware. At Ayious, 0.1 percent are Combed ware, 0.05 percent are Painted-and-Combed ware, and 0.06 percent are Dark Burnished ware. At Kokkinoyia/Pamboules, 0.02 percent are Combed ware sherds and 0.01 percent are Painted-and-Combed; no Dark Burnished ware is present (Table 2-1). There is a corresponding decrease in Red-on-White ware, but the Monochrome category may well include many sherds from painted vessels. Also, 11 percent of the pottery from Tenta, 28.8 percent from Ayious, and 16 percent from Kokkinoyia/Pamboules was so badly desurfaced that it could not be identified by ware type.

Surface Treament

A second factor to consider when attempting to establish a sequence for the three Vasilikos valley sites is the presence or absence of a white slip on Red-on-White ware sherds. Red-on-White ware at Tenta is characterized by the application of the painted decoration directly to the surface of the vessel. At Ayious, Red-on-White ware is generally painted using the same technique, but a white slip is sometimes employed. At Kokkinoyia/Pamboules, a white slip is always present.

Shapes

The vessel shapes present at Tenta, Ayious, and Kokkinoyia/Pamboules become more complex when the sites are considered in this order. Vessel shapes at Tenta are simple. Rims are not articulated, and bases are either round or omphalos in design. Spouts do not occur. At Ayious, the vessel shapes are more developed. There is a variety of rim configurations, and peg bases are found together with round and omphalos types. Tubular spouts and saucers occur in the fine wares at Ayious, and there are flat-bottomed trays with very low rims in Coarse ware. None of these shapes occurs at Tenta. Rims at Kokkinoyia/Pamboules are even more developed, as are the bases, which include both peg and pedestal types. Pierced lug handles are present at Kokkinoyia/Pamboules but not at Tenta or Ayious.

Decoration

A similar development can be traced by comparing the design elements found in the painted patterns on Red-on-White ware sherds from the three sites. In terms of the frequency of selected patterns, the complexity of the designs in general, and the actual painting techniques used, there is a clear development from Tenta through Ayious to Kokkinoyia/Pamboules.

The Tenta ceramics are painted with simple patterns; the lattice pattern does not occur at the site, nor do interlinear dots. The paint is thick and non-penetrating, and the patterns are carefully executed. At Ayious, the patterns are more complex. Not only do such motifs as dots, wavy lines, and overlapping chevrons occur, but single vessels are decorated with a series of different motifs. The workmanship at Ayious is less careful than that at Tenta; the paint, while still non-penetrating, is thinner and tends to run. At Kokkinoyia/Pamboules, the painted patterns are still more complex. Lattice patterns are common, and interlinear dots occur in several different designs. The ceramics from the latter site, however, evidence a new degree of carelessness in the painting of the designs; the thin penetrating paint often runs, causing an extension of the lattice patterns beyond the edges of their areas, leading to development of new decorative motifs.

Constructional Characteristics

Two additional characteristics of the pottery must be considered. Both concern the actual construction of the vessels, and both may be regional, restricted to southern Cyprus. The first of these characteristics is the presence of Fabric A, which seems to be unique to the Vasilikos valley. Fabric A is common at Tenta (77 percent of the total sherds studied and 85 percent of the fine wares) and less common at Ayious (61 percent of the total sherds and 69 percent of the fine wares). At Kokkinoyia/Pamboules, it is not commonly found (13 percent of the total sherds, and 14 percent of the fine wares). There is an obvious decrease in the use of Fabric A from Tenta to Ayious to Kokkinoyia/Pamboules; a concomitant increase (of the total sherds from those sites) may be noted in Fabric B: 13 percent at Tenta, 28 percent at Ayious, and 85 percent at Kokkinoyia/Pamboules.

The second characteristic is the layered construction technique common at Tenta and Ayious, but not found at Kokkinoyia/Pamboules. It seems unlikely that potters would adopt such an obviously laborious construction method unless the properties of the clay at their disposal made it absolutely necessary. As Franken (1971: 237-238) states, all potters are at the mercy of their materials. It is probable that layered construction was connected with the utilization of the clay from which Fabric A was produced, since the two characteristics occur together at Tenta and Ayious and are absent (or essentially so) from Kokkinoyia/Pamboules.

The author sought the assistance of project geologist, Frank Koucky, in locating the clay source for Fabric A. The search was not easy since the entire valley is rich in clays, and there is nothing to indicate that the prehistoric inhabitants necessarily exploited only those clay beds most easily located. After two seasons, Koucky has informed the author of his conclusion that erosion in the valley has been so great since prehistoric times that the clay beds then in use have probably been destroyed. It, therefore, seems unlikely that the continuation of the search will locate the source of the clay employed for Fabric A.

It should be noted that, while the correlation of Fabric A and the layered construction technique seems fairly likely in the Vasilikos valley, multiple-layered construction is not unique to Tenta and Ayious. Layered vessels are found elsewhere in Cyprus in areas where Fabric A does not exist. Dikaios (1961: 172), in describing bowls found at Sotira-Teppes, writes that some vessels have walls "composed of three or four layers of which the outer ones tend to get detached." He also mentioned the occurrence of a naturally light-firing clay at Sotira (ibid.: 179, 181).

Ceramics from Sotira housed in the Cyprus Museum were examined by the author in 1978. Although layered sherds were found, the light fabric in question is not Fabric A. Layered construction is also reported from the Paphos region at

Kissonerga-Mosphilia, but the fabric of these vessels does not resemble Fabric A (personal communication from E.J. Peltenburg). A Red-on-White ware closed vessel from Philia-Drakos A, on display in the Cyprus Museum (ϕ 07 94.4/17), clearly is constructed in three layers, but it too is not made of Fabric A.

Since Fabric B was available to potters at Tenta and Ayious, it is strange that they continued to use Fabric A in view of the construction problems that seem to have been associated with it. The answer may well lie in the potters' ability to apply a light-colored slip over the vessel surface as a background for the red painted patterns. Until the potters developed this ability, they would be forced to utilize Fabric A, at least for all Red-on-White ware vessels. Once they began to use a light-colored slip, it was no longer important for them to have light-colored clay, and the use of Fabric A declined. The available evidence from the Vasilikos valley sites seems to support this common-sense hypothesis.

It should be noted that a similar situation may have existed at Sotira. Stanley Price (1979:69) has observed that Sotira Red-on-White decoration is found only on sherds with a light-colored fabric.[11] He further suggests (ibid.:75) that this light fabric is unlikely to have been available locally, which may account for the scarcity of Red-on-White ware at Sotira (2.6 percent of the total sherds found there) (ibid.: 71 Table 2). It is of interest that, at the northern Sotira culture site of Ayios Epiktitos-Vrysi, potters did apply a light slip to the fabric of Red-on-White ware vessels (Peltenburg 1978: 66 note 36). The ability to produce a light background on a darker clay vessel might then be a determining factor in whether or not a strong tradition of painted decoration developed. Such a suggestion may provide an alternative to the conclusions of Peltenburg (ibid.: 66) who sees the presence or absence of painted decoration (specifically of ripple patterns, which he states are not found in southern Cyprus, but which have now been found at Kalavasos-Tenta) as a matter of cultural trends representing stimulus-diffusion contacts rather than as a local response to technological problems. This question requires further examination, especially as the utilization of a white slip in the Vasilikos valley coincides with painted patterns that are definitely in the Erimi tradition, and therefore indicative of a Chalcolithic date.

COMPARISON OF THE VASILIKOS VALLEY CERAMICS WITH THOSE OF THE SOTIRA AND ERIMI CULTURES

Peltenburg (1978: 66) has recently suggested that the inhabitants of Cyprus during the second half of the fourth millennium B.C. belonged to a single Late Neolithic culture, the Sotira culture, while those living in the succeeding millennium were members of a single unified Chalcolithic culture, the Erimi culture (Peltenburg 1979: 9). It follows, then, that comparison of the Vasilikos valley sites with Sotira and Erimi might help to establish whether the Vasilikos valley sequence is Neolithic, Neolithic-Chalcolithic, or Chalcolithic.

Obvious problems exist with such a comparison. Nonceramic cultural features are outside the scope of this paper, yet such factors as architectural styles and tool types are important in determining the relationship among sites. Moreover, the change from one period to another is seldom marked by a sudden change in artifact types. Nevertheless, it seems necessary to consider how the Vasilikos valley ceramic sequence might fit into the Neolithic/Chalcolithic cultural dichotomy.

Ware Types

According to Stanley Price (1979: 71 Table 2), in all phases at Sotira an almost even division of sherds exists between the two main wares, Red Lustrous and Combed (41 percent and 36.3 percent respectively, of the total wares). At Ayios Epiktitos-Vrysi "almost all the pottery belongs to" Red-on-White ware, or at least bears painted decoration (Peltenburg 1978: 66). Peltenburg (idem) suggests that painted wares in the north and combed wares in the south represent similar stylistic trends equally representative of the Sotira culture. At Tenta, Combed, Painted-and-Combed, and Red-on-White wares combined represent 17 percent of the total pottery, with Red-on-White ware comprising 15 percent of that figure (see Table 2-1). At Ayious, 5.15 percent of the total pottery is represented by the three wares, of which 5 percent is Red-on-White. At Kokkinoyia/Pamboules, 4.03 percent of the total pottery is represented by the three wares, of which 4 percent is Red-on-White. Monochrome ware represents 62 percent of the pottery at Tenta, 55 percent of the pottery at Ayious, and 78 percent of the pottery at Kokkinoyia/Pamboules. These figures do not assist in determining whether the Vasilikos valley sequence is Neolithic or Chalcolithic.

Surface Treatment

The question of the presence or absence of a white slip on the surface of Red-on-White ware vessels was considered earlier. It may be useful to mention briefly its presence or absence on other wares from the sites under consideration. At Sotira, some Combed ware vessels and some Red Lustrous ware (Dikaios 1961: 179, 181) are reported to bear a white slip. No evidence appears for the use of a white slip at Tenta, and it is very rare at Ayious. The white slip occurs on all the fine wares at Kokkinoyia/Pamboules. At Erimi it is common, and Stewart (1978: 12, 13), describing Chalcolithic period ceramics from the Paphos region, reports the presence of a white slip on Red Monochrome Painted and Red-on-White wares. It would seem that whereas the presence or absence of the white slip may be a useful developmental marker for a given region, by itself it is not helpful in determining the cultural period of a single site.

Shapes

Peltenburg (1978: 66) has stated that the shapes and sizes of Sotira culture ceramics in the north and south of Cyprus are identical. As he illustrated (1978: 60 fig. 3), Sotira culture pottery consists mainly of flat and round-bottomed bowls and flat and round-bottomed jugs with vertical necks. These shapes are essentially identical to those from Kalavasos "A" published by Dikaios (1962: 109 fig. 53). Tenta pottery shapes bear some similarities to those from Kalavasos "A," but spouted bowls, common at Sotira culture sites, do not occur at Tenta. Two shallow trays with drain (?) holes above the base (see note 6), have been found at Tenta similar to those excavated at Ayios Epiktitos-Vrysi. A similar sherd was found at Kokkinoyia/Pamboules.

Vessel shapes at Kalavasos-Ayious and Kalavasos-Kokkinoyia/Pamboules are essentially the same, the ceramics of the latter site apparently representing a development from those of the former site. Shapes from these sites most closely resemble those published by Dikaios from Kalavasos "A" and Kalavasos "B" (Dikaios 1962: 109 fig. 53; 137 fig. 64), although parallels with Erimi occur at Kokkinoyia/Pamboules. The shapes of both Ayious and Kokkinoyia/Pamboules ceramics are paralleled in the Paphos region, the most interesting similarity being provided by the "saucer" shape (found in fine ware at Ayious and Coarse ware at Kokkinoyia/Pamboules) similar to

Table 2-1. Ware percentages of total earlier prehistoric ceramics from each site.

| Site | Monochrome | | Red-on-White | | Combed | | Painted-and-Combed | | Dark Burnished Ware | Coarse Ware | Desurfaced |
	Open	Closed	Open	Closed	Open	Closed	Open	Closed			
TENTA	20%	42%	5%	10%	0.4%	1%	0.4%	0.2%	1%	9%	11%
AYIOUS	12%	43%	1%	4%	0.02%	0.08%	0.01%	0.04%	0.06%	11%	28.8%
KOKKINOYIA/ PAMBOULES	42%	36%	2%	2%	0.01%	0.01%	0.01%	---	---	2%	16%

The terms "open" and "closed" refer to the shapes of the vessels.

the example illustrated by Peltenburg (see note 8).

Decoration

In the area of decoration, the ceramic material from the three Vasilikos valley sites can be compared most directly to Sotira or Erimi culture pottery. Both Combed and Painted-and-Combed wares are rare in the Vasilikos valley, and those few examples found are fragmentary. Therefore, a discussion of decoration must be limited to Red-on-White ware painted patterns.

The primary question is whether the Vasilikos valley Red-on-White wares belong to the bold (i.e., Neolithic) or thin-line (i.e., Chalcolithic) type. The painted patterns found at Tenta resemble, to a limited degree, those found at Sotira, but they do not resemble at all those from Troulli and Ayios Epiktitos-Vrysi, except in the actual painting technique. This is a much more careful technique than that found at Sotira and resembles the painting employed at the north coast sites.

The painted patterns from Ayious have affinities with both the Sotira culture and the Erimi culture material. The patterns are closer to the latter in design, but they resemble the former in boldness. Two of the more unusual Ayious designs have direct parallels at Erimi. The sherd from Ayious decorated with blobs of paint (Figure 2-11: 3) is similar to examples from Erimi (Dikaios 1936: pl. XXI: 19, 36; pl. XXII: 19), and the zigzag and wavy lines of Ayious also resemble those from the latter site (ibid.: pl. XIX: 2, 18, 23; pl. XX: 1, 13, 18, 21).

Many close parallels exist between the decorative motifs of Kokkinoyia/Pamboules and Erimi. Kokkinoyia/Pamboules lattice patterns are directly in the Erimi artistic tradition. The use of extended lines is found at Erimi, as are the patterns that developed from these extended lines. For example, the pattern found at Kokkinoyia/ Pamboules (Figure 2-15:5) consisting of a triangular area filled with diagonal lattice and finished at the lowest corner with a pair of thick strokes, is directly paralleled at Erimi (ibid.: pl. XXI: 20, 39; pl. XXIII: 17; pl. XXIV).

There is no evidence for pure Sotira culture bold Red-on-White decoration at any of the three Vasilikos valley sites, although some similarities to it have been found at Tenta and Ayious. The Red-on-White ware of Kokkinoyia/Pamboules seems clearly to belong to the Erimi tradition.

CONCLUSIONS

A picture of steady development emerges from this study of the earlier prehistoric pottery from Tenta, Ayious, and Kokkinoyia/Pamboules. The earliest material, from Tenta, seems to fall stylistically at the very end of the ceramic Neolithic period. Perhaps the ceramic levels at Tenta fit in the gap mentioned by Peltenburg (1979: 11) between the end of the Sotira culture and the beginning of the Erimi culture, in which case they might be termed "Proto-Chalcolithic" or simply Early Chalcolithic. The Ayious ceramics clearly have attributes from both the Sotira and Erimi cultures, but the closer affinities are with the Chalcolithic. The ceramic material from Kokkinoyia/Pamboules is clearly Chalcolithic in the Erimi tradition. Thus, the three sites represent a developmental sequence in the Chalcolithic period. It is hoped that the Vasilikos valley will eventually prove to have been occupied from the aceramic Neolithic through the end of the Chalcolithic period, and that this ceramic sequence, established for the moment at three sites, can be expanded in time back to the origins of pottery in the area and forward through the transition to the Early Bronze Age.

NOTES

1. The processing of the ceramics consisted of describing the sherds macroscopically. Within each processed group, every sherd was assigned a ware type (see note 4) based on surface treatment; a fabric type based on the clay body; and, whenever possible, given the badly abraded nature of much of the material, a shape category – initially simply the broad divisions of "open" and "closed." Both surface and fabric color(s) were recorded for a random selection of sherds using the Munsell color notation system. Each group of sherds was weighed and counted to minimize the problems resulting from relying on either counting or weighing as the sole bulk measurement method. Diagnostic sherds were individually measured, drawn, and Munsell color coded.

   Where possible, construction and firing technique data were recorded. The need for developing pottery typologies based on more precise categories than the traditional division according to shape and surface treatment is obvious (cf. Franken 1971: 227ff). Unfortunately, both the fragmentary nature of the ceramics themselves, and their sometimes disturbed contexts, have made this only partially possible so far.

2. This "thin-line" Red-on-White painted ware is so described in comparison with the earlier and bolder Red-on-White painted pottery found by Dikaios in the first ceramic levels at Troulli. Peltenburg (1978: 66-68) has identified this bolder Red-on-White as one of the two major ceramic styles indicating the presence of the Sotira culture, a term he employs to describe a Late Neolithic culture represented at Sotira, Ayios Epiktitos-Vrysi, Troulli, Philia-Drakos A, and in one pit from Dikaios' Kalavasos "B" (Dikaios 1962: 198, fig. XLII:4).

3. All numerical notations following color descriptions refer to the Munsell color notation system.

4. Dikaios' use of the term "ware" designates a pottery type defined principally on the basis of surface decoration with little reference to the fabric (Dikaios 1961: 172ff). Although his terminology is not ideal and is, indeed, in the process of modification (Stewart 1978), it has been employed here whenever practical, in an attempt to simplify comparative analysis. However, whereas such wares as Combed and Red-on-White are easily distinguishable, Dikaios' categories of Red Lustrous, Red Slip, Grey Lustrous, Black Lustrous, and Plain White are impossible to differentiate in fragmentary and unevenly fired material. Further, the validity of these types is open to question. Stanley Price (1979:69), for example, has identified Red Slip as a variant of Red Lustrous, and future studies may well result in a further reduction in the number of identifiable separate monochrome types.

5. For further description of the Dark Burnished ware, see Kromholz 1979: 38.

6. Peltenburg (1978: 72 and 73 fig. 7) identifies similar trays with olive oil production.

7.   For details of the excavation of square C 11 C, see Todd et al. 1979a: 26ff; Todd et al. 1979b: 281–282.

8.   A similar vessel from Kissonerga-Mosphilia is illustrated by Peltenburg (1979:31 fig. 10:9), and another was found at Lemba-Lakkous according to a personal communication from J. Stewart.

9.   For the initial publication of the site, see Dikaios 1962: 106ff and 133ff. Notes on the site are also to be found in Todd 1977: 29; Todd et al. 1978: 186; Todd et al. 1979b: 284–285.

10. While the ceramic changes are deemed to be of chronological significance, future analyses pertaining to the nature of the three sites may indicate other factors that must be considered. Analyses of the excavated data from Ayious are in a preliminary stage, the Kokkinoyia/Pamboules material was obtained by surface collection rather than by excavation, and it is at present impossible to estimate the significance of economic and environmental factors with reference to ceramic change.

11. Note that Dikaios (1961:181) describes the vessel surface of Red-on-White ware as being smoothed to resemble a slip or covered with a light-colored slip.

ACKNOWLEDGMENTS

This material is based upon work supported by the National Science Foundation under Grants no. BNS76-12313, BNS76-12313 AO1, BNS77-07685, and BNS77-07685 AO1-02.

***

I should like to thank Dr. Ian A. Todd for his permission to study and publish the earlier prehistoric ceramics from the Vasilikos valley, and also for his unfailing help and encouragement both in Cyprus and across half the globe. I should also like to express my gratitude to Dr. Vassos Karageorghis, Director of the Department of Antiquities of the Republic of Cyprus, for permission to study the Erimi and Sotira ceramics in the Cyprus Museum; to Dr. Ino Nicolaou for expediting my work in the Museum; and to the Museum staff who aided me in locating the material in question. I would further like to thank Dr. E.J. Peltenburg and Jennifer Stewart for valuable discussion about the Vasilikos valley and the Paphos area ceramics, and Paul Croft and Alice Kingsnorth, staff members of the Vasilikos Valley Project, for their advice and encouragement.

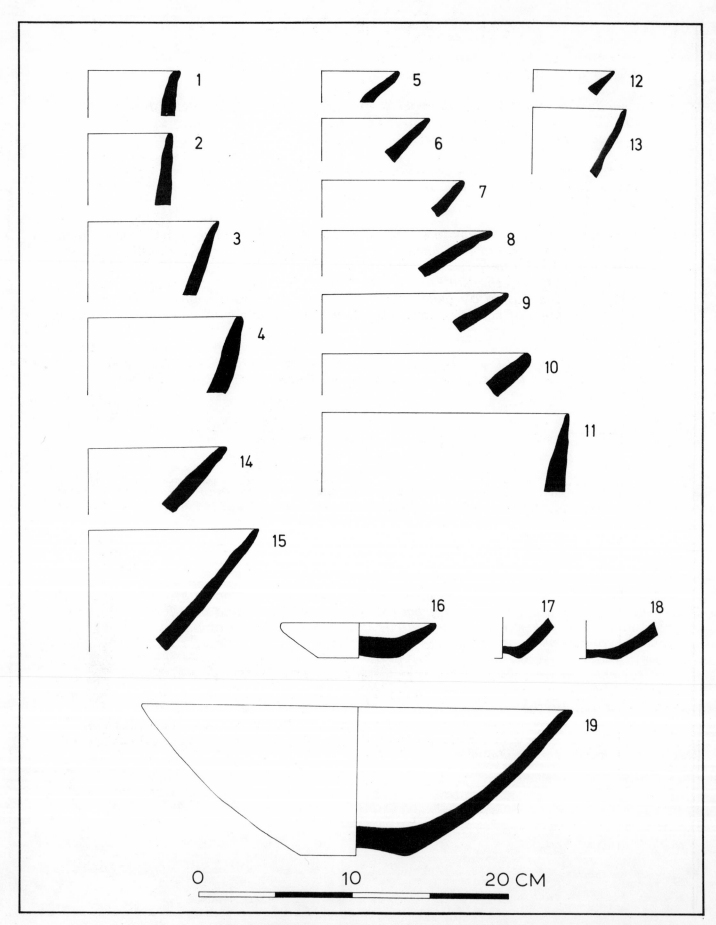

2-1. Kalavasos-Tenta: Fine ware open shapes (Monochrome: 1, 2, 5-8, 10-13, 15-19; Red-on-White: 3, 4, 9, 14). Drawn by Paul Rehak from original drawings by Susan Kromholz.

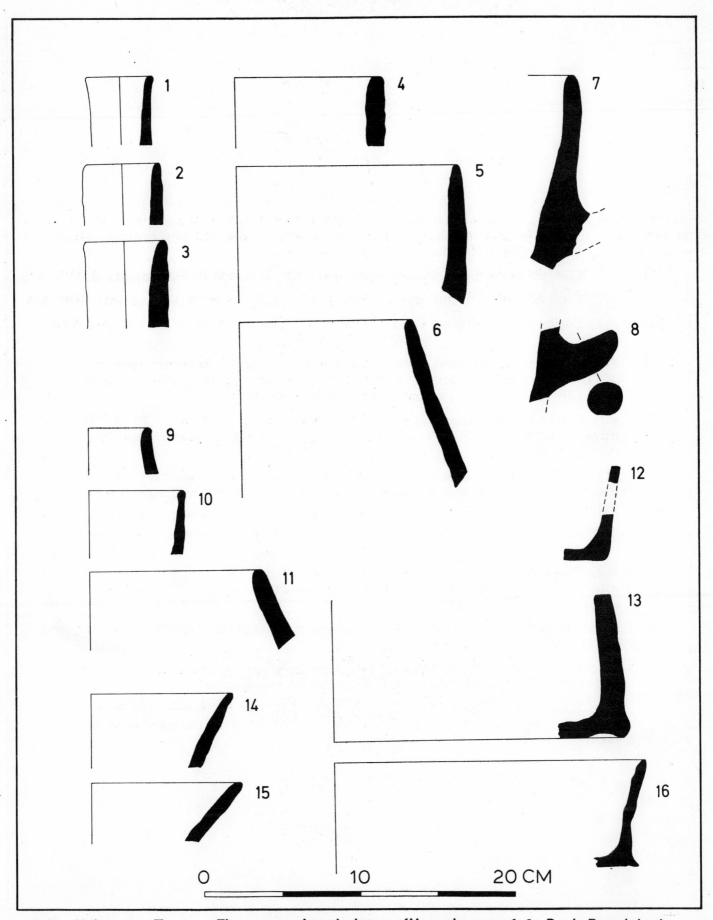

2-2. Kalavasos-Tenta: Fine ware closed shapes (Monochrome: 1-3; Dark Burnished: 4-8; Coarse: 9-16). Drawn by Paul Rehak from original drawings by Susan Kromholz.

2-3.   Kalavasos-Tenta: Ceramics excavated in 1978 in sounding in square 0 16 B. The two-digit number preceding each description indicates the deposit number within the square.   Drawn by Paul Rehak.

1)   2.2; Combed ware open shape; Fabric B; fabric: 7.5YR 6/5; paint: 2.5YR 3/5.

2)   2.2; Combed ware closed shape; Fabric B; fabric: 2.5YR 6/5; paint: 1OR 4/4.

3)   7.1; Combed ware closed shape; Fabric B; fabric: 10YR 7.5/4; paint: 5YR 3.5/3.

4)   7.I; Painted-and-Combed ware open shape; Fabric A; interior fabric: 7.5YR 6/5; exterior fabric: 7.5YR 7.5/2; interior paint:5YR 4/5; exterior paint: 2.5YR 3.5/4; pattern slightly reconstructed.

5)   6.I; Painted-and-Combed ware open shape; Fabric B; fabric: 10YR 7/4; interior paint: 2.5YR 3/5; exterior paint: 10R 5/6; pattern slightly reconstructed.

6)   6.1; Painted-and-Combed ware open shape; Fabric B; fabric: 2.5YR 6/4; interior paint: 2.5YR 3/4; exterior: originally combed but very worn.

7)   5.1; Painted-and-Combed ware open shape; Fabric B; fabric: 7.5YR 7.5/4; interior paint: 2.5YR 3.5/5; exterior paint: 5YR 4/4; pattern slightly reconstructed.

8)   2.2; Painted-and-Combed ware open shape; Fabric B; fabric: 5YR 6/6; interior paint: (one large vertical stripe width 2.8 cm.) 5YR 4.5/4; exterior paint: 5YR 5/4.

9)   8.1; Painted-and-Combed ware closed shape; Fabric B; fabric: 5YR 7/4 and 7.5YR 7/5; paint: 5YR 4.5/4.

10)   7.1; Painted-and-Combed ware open shape; Fabric B; fabric: 10YR 6/3; interior paint: 2.5YR 3/2; exterior surface missing.

11)   3.1; Painted-and-Combed ware open shape; Fabric B; fabric: 10YR 6/4; interior paint: 2.5YR 3/4; exterior paint: 2.5YR 3/4; pattern slightly reconstructed.

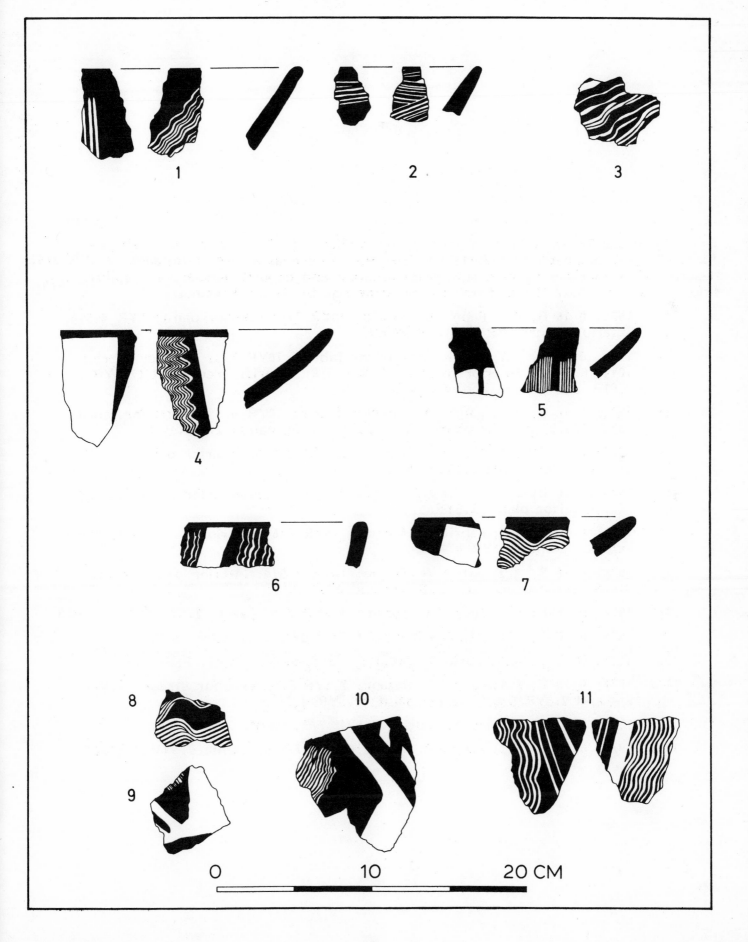

2-4. Kalavasos-Tenta: Red-on-White ware open shapes (1-7, 11) and closed shapes (8-10, 12, 13) excavated in 1976-1978. The year of excavation preceding each description is followed by grid square designation and deposit number. + = surface find. Drawn by Paul Rehak from original drawings by Susan Kromholz.

1)   1978; 0 16 B; 4.1; Fabric B; fabric: 10YR 7/4; interior paint: 5YR 4-5/6; exterior paint: 5YR 4/3.5; mended.

2)   1978; 0 16 B; 4.1; Fabric A; interior fabric: 10YR 7/3; exterior fabric: 10YR 6.5/2.5; interior paint: 2.5YR 4.5/6; exterior: red band (2.5YR 4/6) width 3.6 cm. and over rim.

3)   1978; 0 16 B; 3.2; Fabric A; interior fabric: 10YR 6.5/3; exterior fabric: 10YR 7.5/3; interior paint: 5YR 4/5; exterior paint: 2.5YR 4/5.

4)   1978; 0 16 B; 3.2; Fabric A; fabric: 7.5YR 6.5/4; interior paint: 2.5YR 3/6; exterior paint: 2.5YR 4/4.

5)   1978; 0 16 B; 5.1; Fabric A; fabric: 7.5YR 7.5/3; interior paint: 2.5YR 5/6; exterior plain: 2.5YR 5/6.

6)   1978; 0 16 B; 3.1; Fabric A; fabric: 7.5YR 7/6; interior very badly worn; exterior paint: 2.5YR 4/7.

7)   1978; 0 16 B; 3.2; Fabric A; fabric: 10YR 7.5/4; interior paint: 2.5YR 4.5/6; exterior mottled: 5YR 5/5 and 10YR 4/2.

8)   1978; 0 16 B; 5.1; Fabric A; fabric: 7.5YR 7/4; paint: 2.5YR 3/5.

9)   1978; 0 16 B; 5.1/6.1; Fabric A; fabric: 10YR 7/4; paint: 5YR 4.5/5.

10)   1977; B 7 C; 2.5; Fabric A; fabric: 7.5YR 6.5/4; paint: 7.5R 4/4.

11)   1978; 0 16 B; 5.1; Fabric A; fabric: 7.5YR 8/3; exterior streaky 7.5YR 5/4 and 2.5YR 5/5; interior paint: 2.5YR 4/6.

12)   1976; B 12; +; Fabric A; fabric: 7.5YR 7/3; paint: 2.5YR 3/4.

13)   1978; 0 16 B; 6.1; Fabric A; fabric: 10YR 7/2.5; paint: 2.5YR 4.5/6.

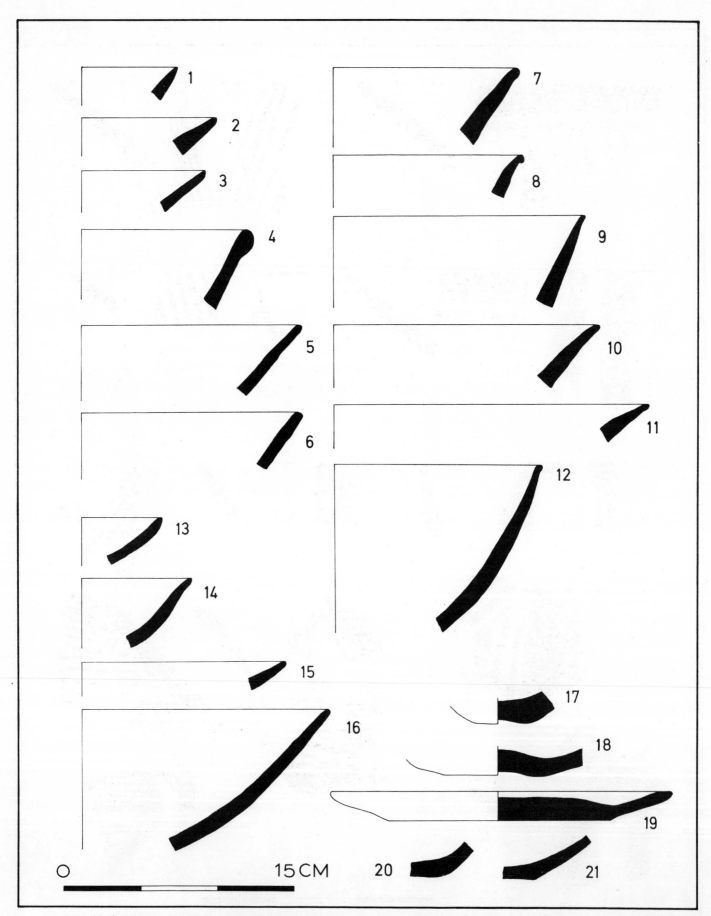

2–5. Kalavasos-Ayious: Fine ware open shapes (Monochrome: 1, 2, 4, 7–9, 11–15, 17, 20; Red-on-White: 3, 5, 6, 10, 16, 21). Drawn by Paul Rehak from original drawings by Susan Kromholz.

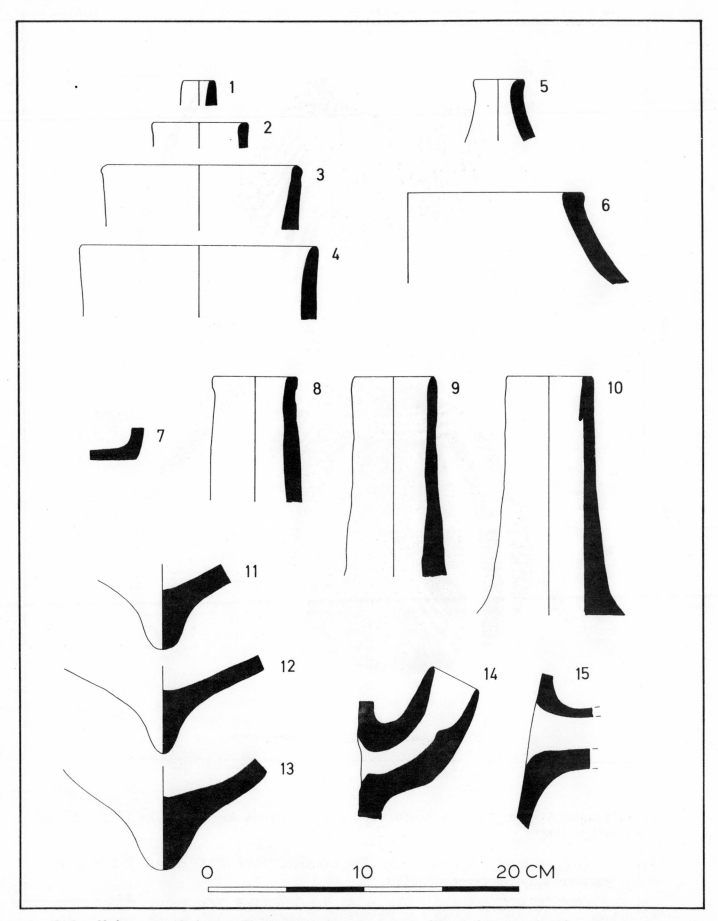

2-6. Kalavasos-Ayious: Fine ware closed shapes (Monochrome: 1-15). Drawn by Paul Rehak from original drawings by Susan Kromholz.

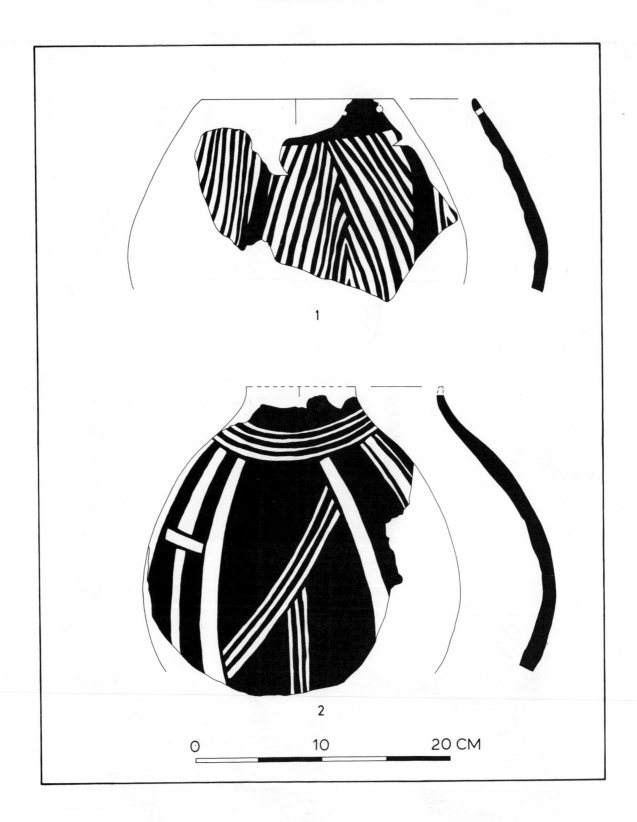

2-7. **Kalavasos-Ayious**: Red-on-White ware closed shapes excavated in 1978. Drawn by Jane Grenville.

1) C 11 C: S.W.Q.; 5.1-5.2; Fabric A; fabric: 10YR 7/3; paint: 2.5YR 5/6; pattern slightly reconstructed.

2) C 11 C: S.W.Q.; 5.2-5.3; Fabric A; fabric: 10YR 7/3; paint: 5YR 4.5/5.

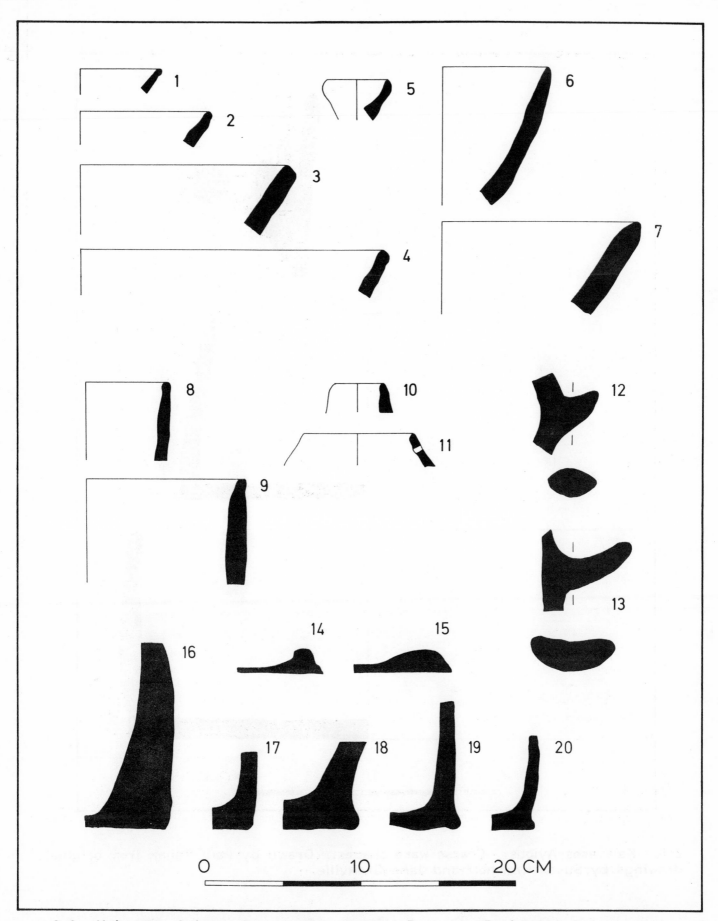

2-8. Kalavasos-Ayious: Coarse ware shapes. Drawn by Paul Rehak from original drawings by Susan Kromholz and Jane Grenville.

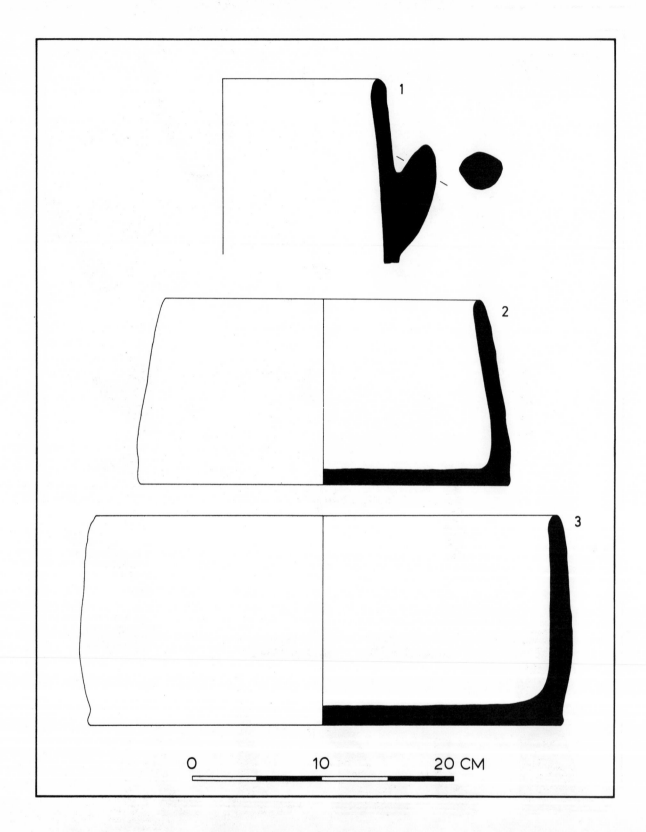

2-9. **Kalavasos-Ayious: Coarse ware shapes. Drawn by Paul Rehak from original drawings by Susan Kromholz and Jane Grenville.**

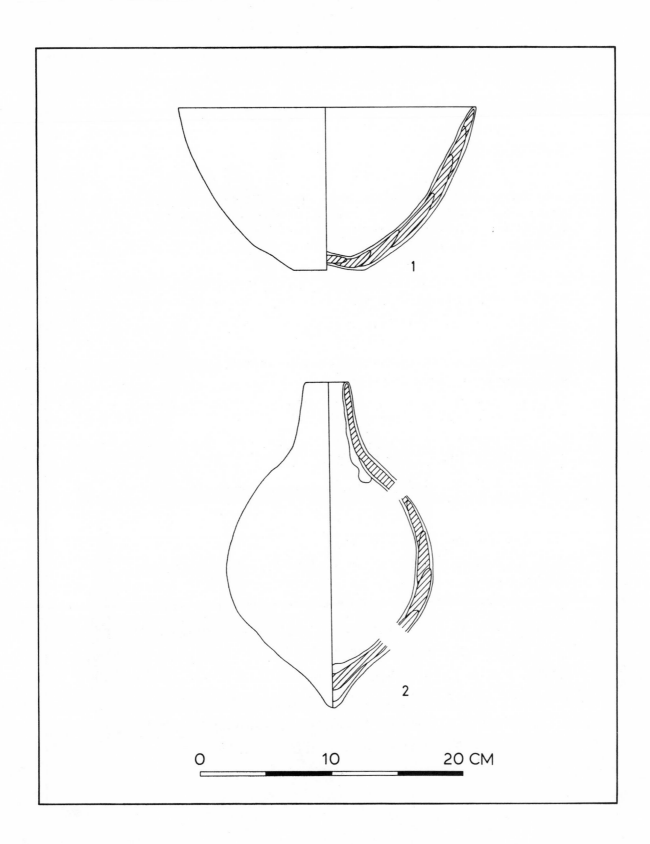

2-10. Kalavasos-Ayious: Illustration of construction techniques. Drawn by Paul Rehak from original drawings by Susan Kromholz.

2-11. Kalavasos-Ayious: Red-on-White ware open shapes (1-7) and closed shapes (8-15) excavated or collected in 1978. The grid square designation (including quadrant where applicable) preceding each description is followed by the deposit number. + = surface find. Most patterns are slightly reconstructed. Drawn by Paul Rehak.

1) C 11 C; N.W.Q.; 5.1; Fabric A; fabric: 10YR 8/2.5; interior paint: 5YR 5/5; exterior plain: 5YR 5/5.

2) C 11 C; S.W.Q.; 5.1; Fabric A; fabric: 7.5YR 7/4; interior paint: 2.5YR 5/6; exterior plain: 2.5YR 5/6.

3) (1979); C 11 C; 6.I; Fabric A; fabric: 10YR 7/2; interior paint: 2.5YR 4.5/5; exterior plain (matt): 2.5YR 4.5/5.

4) C 11 C; S.W.Q.; 5.1; Fabric A; fabric: 7.5YR 7/4; interior plain: 7.5YR 7/4; exterior paint: 2.5YR 4.5/6.

5) C 11 C; N.W.Q.; 5.2; Fabric B; fabric: 5YR 7/4; interior paint: 2.5YR 3/2; exterior plain: 2.5YR 3.5/4.

6) C 11 C; S.W.Q.; 5.1; Fabric A; fabric: 10YR 7/4; interior paint: 2.5YR 4/6; exterior plain: 2.5YR 4/6.

7) C 11 C; S.W.Q.; 5.3; Fabric A; fabric: 10YR 8/3; interior plain: 7.5YR 2/0; exterior paint: 2.5YR 5/6.

8) C 11 C; S.W.Q.; 5.1; Fabric A; fabric: 7.5YR 8/2; paint: 2.5YR 4/4 and 7.5YR 3/0.

9) B 2; +; Fabric A; fabric: 7.5YR 8/4; paint: 10R 5/4.

10) C 11 C; N.W.Q.; 5.1; Fabric A; fabric: 10YR 8/2; paint: 5YR 4/4.

11) C 11 C; S.W.Q.; 5.1; Fabric A; fabric: 10YR 7/3; paint: 5YR 5.5/6.

12) C 11 C; N.W.Q.; 5.2; Fabric B; fabric: 10YR 7/2; paint: 2.5YR 4.5/5.

13) B 6; +; Fabric A; fabric: 7.5YR 8/3; paint: 2.5YR 4/5.

14) D 2; +; Fabric A; fabric: 10YR 7/2.5; paint: 5YR 4/4.

15) C 11 C; N.W.Q.; 5.1; Fabric B; fabric: 7.5YR 7.5/2; paint: 2.5YR 3/6.

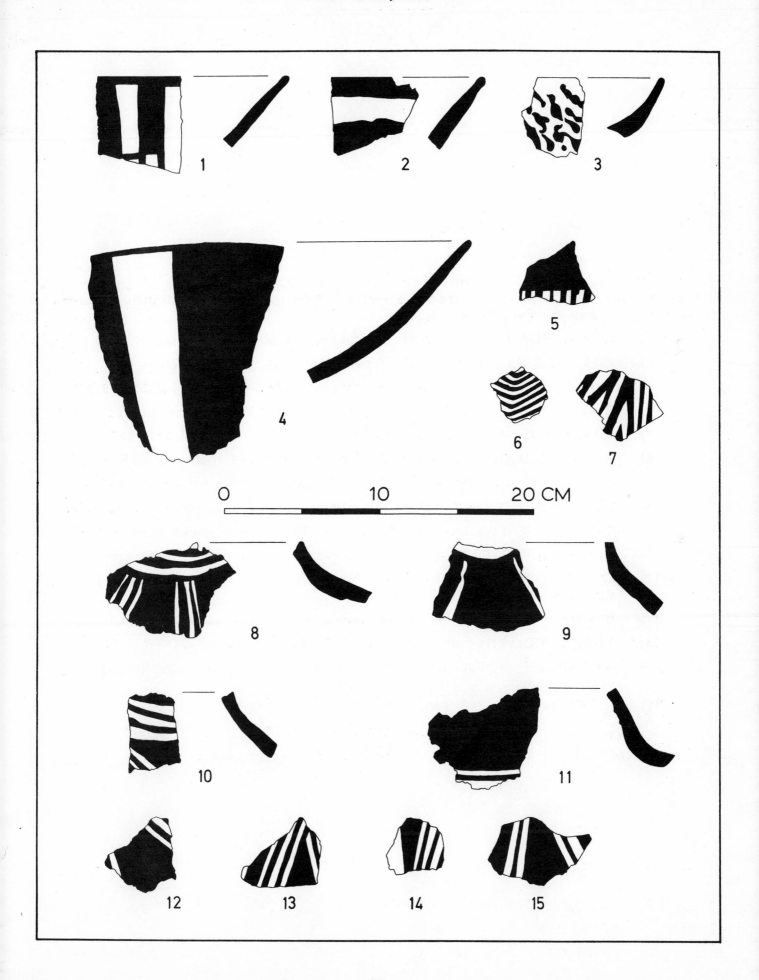

2-12. Kalavasos-Ayious: Red-on-White ware closed shapes (1-11, 13-17) and neck (12) excavated in 1978 unless otherwise stated. Most patterns are slightly reconstructed. Drawn by Paul Rehak.

1) C 11 C; N.W.Q.; 5.2; Fabric A; fabric: 10YR 8/2; paint: 5YR 4/4.

2) 1979; C 9 C; 3.1; Fabric A; fabric: 10YR 7/2; paint: 5YR 4/4.

3) C 11 C; N.W.Q.; 5.1; Fabric B; fabric: 10YR 7/3; paint: 2.5YR 3.5/5.

4) C 11 C; N.W.Q.; 5.1; Fabric A; fabric: 10YR 7.5/2.5; paint: 2.5YR 5/5.

5) 1979; C 9 C; 4.1; Fabric B; fabric: 7.5YR 6/4; paint: 2.5YR 4/6.

6) C 11 C; S.W.Q.; 5.2; Fabric A; fabric: 10YR 7/3; paint: 2.5YR 3.5/6.

7) D 7; +; Fabric A; fabric: 10YR 7/2.5; paint: 2.5YR 4/5 - 5YR 4/3.5.

8) C 11 C; N.W.Q.; 5.1; Fabric A; fabric: 10YR 7.5/3; paint: 2.5YR 4/7.

9) C 11 C; S.W.Q; 5.2; Fabric A; fabric: 10YR 7.5/3; paint: 2.5YR 4.5/6.

10) C 11 C; S.W.Q.; 5.1; Fabric B; fabric 10YR 8/4; paint: 5YR 3.5/2.5.

11) C 11 C; S.W.Q.; 5.2; Fabric B; fabric: 7.5YR 7/5; paint: 10R 4/5 (possible slip).

12) B 6 D; S.E.Q.; 5.1; Fabric A; fabric: 7.5YR 7/4; paint: 10R 4/6.

13) 1979; C 9 C; 4.1; Fabric B; fabric: 7.5YR 7/4; paint: 2.5YR 3.5/5.

14) West slope 7; +; Fabric A; fabric: 7.5YR 6.5/4; paint: 2.5YR 4/4; very worn, mended.

15) B 6 D; S.W.Q.; 2.1; Fabric B; slip: 7.5YR 7/3; paint: 7.5R 4/4.

16) C 11 C; N.W.Q.; 5.1; Fabric A; fabric: 10YR 7/3; paint: 2.5YR 4/5.

17) 1979; C 9 C; 3.1; Fabric B; fabric: 5YR 7/3.5; paint: 2.5YR 4.5/6.

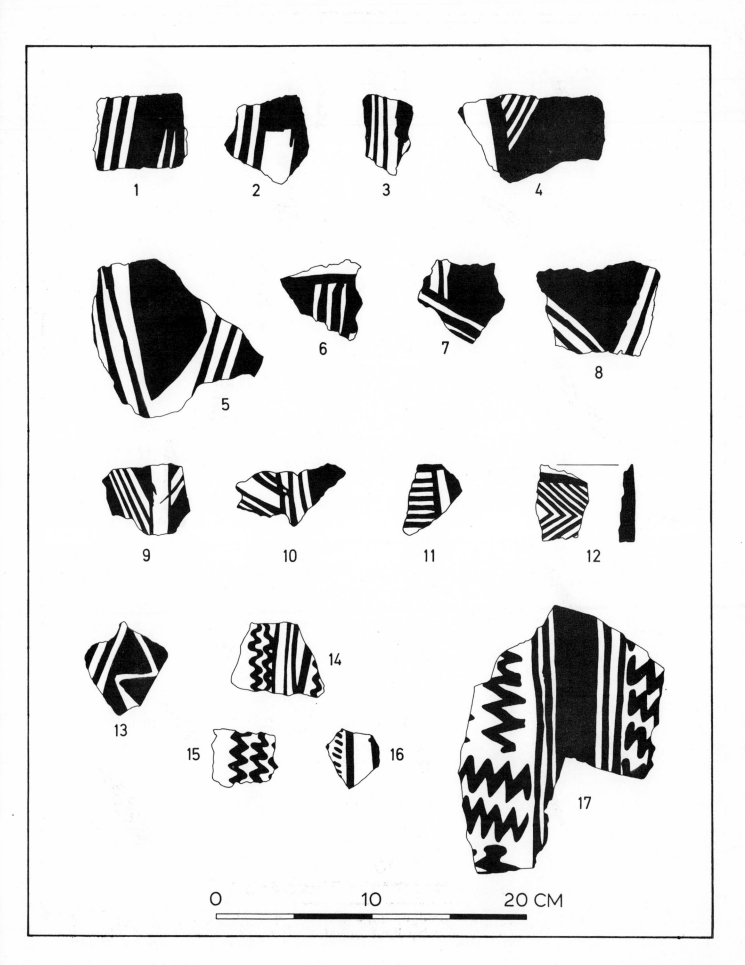

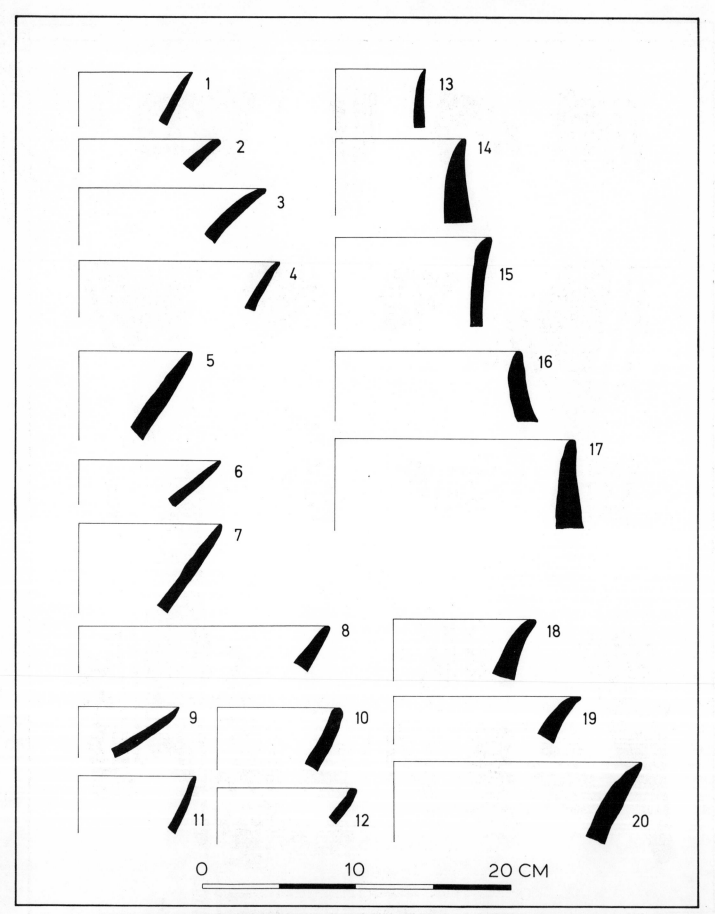

2-13. Kalavasos-Kokkinoyia/Pamboules: Fine ware open shapes (Monochrome: 1-17, 19; Red-on-White: 18, 20). Drawn by Paul Rehak from original drawings by Susan Kromholz.

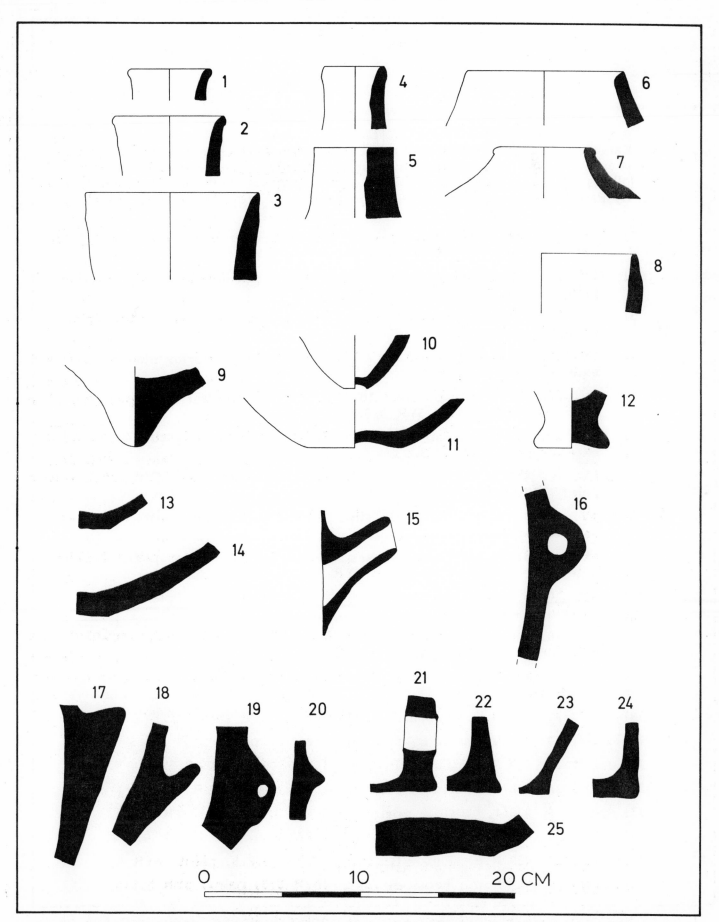

2-14. Kalavasos-Kokkinoyia/Pamboules: Fine ware closed shapes (Monochrome: 1-16) and Coarse ware shapes (17-25). Drawn by Paul Rehak from original drawings by Susan Kromholz and Paul Rehak.

2-15. Kalavasos-Kokkinoyia/Pamboules: Red-on-White ware open shapes (1-12) and closed shapes (13-20) collected from the surface in 1976. The description of the sherd follows the Cadastral Plan reference. Most patterns are slightly reconstructed. Drawn by Paul Rehak from original drawings by Susan Kromholz and Paul Rehak.

1) LV. 20. 439; Coarse fabric; slip: 10YR 7.5/2; interior plain: 5YR 5.5/4; exterior paint: 2.5YR 5/7.

2) LV. 20. 439; Fabric B; slip: 10YR 8/3; interior totally worn; exterior paint: 2.5YR 4/5.

3) LV. 20. 439 N.W.; Fabric B; slip: 7.5YR 7.5/2; interior totally worn; exterior paint: 2.5YR 5/6.

4) LV. 20. 439 N.W.; Fabric B; slip: 7.5YR 7.5/3; interior plain: 2.5YR 4/6; exterior paint: 2.5YR 5/6.

5) LV. 20. 439; Fabric B; slip: 10YR 7.5/3; interior worn but probably plain red; exterior paint: 2.5YR 3/6.

6) LV. 20. 439 N.W.; Fabric B; slip: 10YR 7/2; interior plain: 2.5YR 6/6; exterior paint: 5YR 4/3.

7) LV. 20. 438/2; Fabric B; slip: 2.5Y 8/2; interior plain: 5YR 3/2; exterior paint: 5YR 4/6.

8) LV. 20. 439 N.W.; Fabric B; slip: 10YR 8/4; interior paint: 10R 3.5/7; exterior worn.

9) LV. 20. 439 N.E.; Fabric B; slip: 7.5YR 7.5/4; interior plain: 2.5YR 5/6; exterior paint: 2.5YR 4/5 and 5YR 5/8.

10) LV. 20. 439 NW.; Fabric B; slip: 10YR 7.5/4; interior plain: 7.5YR 5/6; exterior paint: 7.5YR 5/6.

11) LV. 20. 438/4; Fabric B; slip: 10YR 7.5/3.5; interior plain: 10YR 7.5/3.5; exterior paint: 5YR 4/5.

12) LV. 20. 439 N.W.; Fabric B; slip: 10YR 8/3; interior worn; exterior paint: 2.5YR 4.5/6.

13) LV. 20. 439 N.W.; Fabric B; slip: 10YR 7.5/4; paint: 2.5YR 5/6.

14) LV. 20. 438/4; Fabric B; slip: 10YR 8/2.5; paint: 5YR 3/2.5.

15) LV. 20. 439 N.W.; Fabric B; slip: 10YR 7/2; paint: 7.5YR 4/4.

16) LV. 20. 438/2; Fabric B; slip: 10YR 7/3; paint: 5YR 3/3.

17) LV. 20. 438/1; Fabric A; paint: 10R 4.5/6; fabric: 10YR 7.5/3.

18) LV. 20. 439; Fabric A; fabric: 10YR 7/2.5; paint: 7.5YR 4.5/4.

19) LV. 20. 439 N.E.; Fabric B; slip: 10YR 7.5/2.5; paint: 5YR 4/6.

20) LV. 20. 439 N.W.; Fabric B; slip: 10YR 8/3; paint: 5YR 5.5/6.

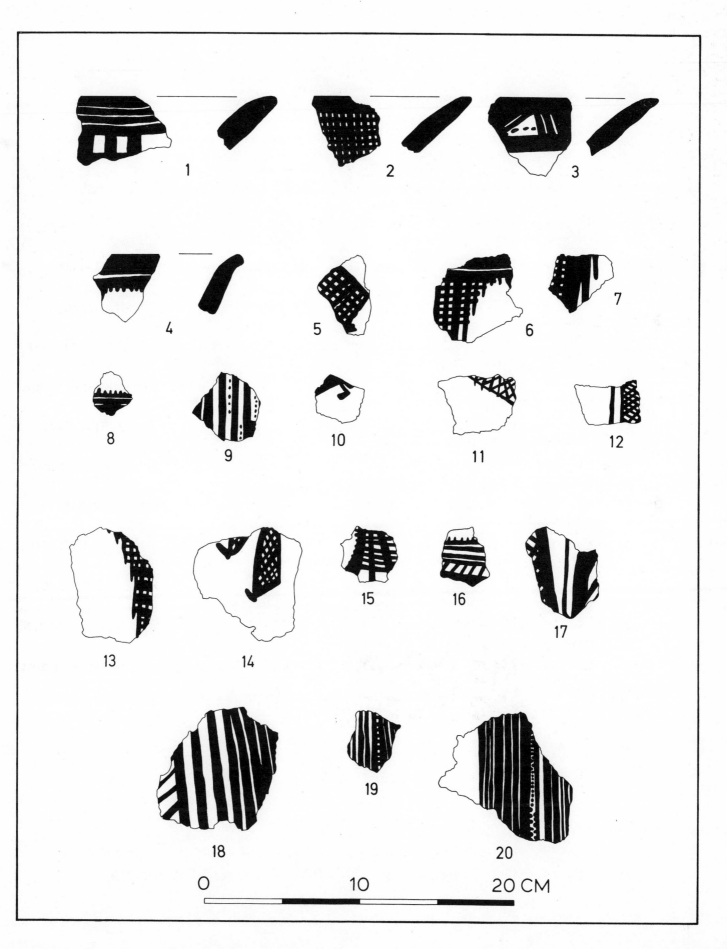

Part II

Phaneromeni

CHAPTER 3.

EXCAVATIONS AT PHANEROMENI: 1975-1978

James R. Carpenter

The site of Phaneromeni lies east of the village of Episkopi, near the southern coast of Cyprus, approximately 14 km. west of Limassol (see frontispiece). It is bordered on the north and west by the Limassol-Paphos highway, on the east by the Kouris River, and on the south by a dirt road leading from the village to the river. Figure 3-1 shows the extent of Kent State University's excavations during recent years (Karageorghis 1976: 872-875; 1977: 746-747; 1978a: 911-913), as well as the location of most of the trial trenches (indicated by the Tr numbers) excavated by Saul S. Weinberg for the University of Missouri in 1955 (Weinberg 1956: 112-121).

The aim in undertaking more extensive excavations at Phaneromeni was to provide new and significant information concerning various problems in Cypriote Bronze Age archaeology. Few excavations of settlements dating from the Early, Middle, and Late Cypriote IA periods had been conducted in Cyprus. Consequently, architectural data from these periods was deficient. Perhaps even more important, Cypriote Bronze Age ceramic typologies were based almost entirely on funerary material and little was known about possible regional variations. Indeed, the use of ceramic typologies based solely on tomb material has led to the misdating of some Bronze Age sites on the island.

The second goal was to develop sound lithic, metal, and terracotta typologies which could be used to classify comparable material from other sites and perhaps be used, also in conjunction with ceramic typologies, as chronological indicators.

The third endeavor was to expand knowledge of Bronze Age settlement patterns in southern Cyprus through systematic surface surveys in the area (Swiny 1981).

The principal Bronze Age remains at Phaneromeni (Figure 3-1) consist of a Middle Bronze Age settlement in Area G; a Middle Bronze Age necropolis in Areas C ("Necropolis" on the plan) and J (not indicated on the plan, but in the vicinity of "56 Km.," in the western portion of the site) and extending into the eastern edge of the village of Episkopi west of the Limassol-Paphos highway; and a settlement of the Late Cypriote IA period in Areas A and J. Tombs contemporary with the Late Cypriote IA settlement were not located in spite of intensive surface reconnaissance in the area of Phaneromeni and extending well into Episkopi. This paper is confined to

Areas G, C (Necropolis), and A.

The Middle Bronze Age settlement in Area G (Figure 3-1) lies east of a Moslem cemetery. In spite of large quantities of stone artifacts and sherds discovered during surface reconnaissance of this and adjoining fields, only fragmentary architectural remains were recovered and only in Trench G4 (Figure 3-2). The best preserved wall (W-A), two courses high and 0.75 m. wide, was built of riverstones and a few irregularly shaped *havara* (Elliott and Dutton 1963: 75-76) blocks. Another partially preserved wall (W-B) probably joined W-A on the latter's eastern side. W-C may be a continuation of W-A. Several mud brick fragments were recovered from the debris, indicating that the superstructure of the walls above the stone foundations was of this material. Clearly definable floor surfaces were rare in Trench G4 (Figure 3-2) (as also in Area A discussed below), but numerous features and artifacts were found in situ on the habitation surface, especially in Areas 1 and 2, including a post support (Ft. 5), mortars (Fts. 3 and 7), an andesite bowl (S251), and an extremely important bifacial gaming stone (S244).

The fragmentary architectural remains are similar in form and construction to those in Area A. Possible parallels for the Bronze Age architecture at Phaneromeni are discussed below.

Pottery found in situ in Area G included fragments of a Red Polished III Mottled amphora (Ft. 1), fragments of a storage jar (Ft. 2), and two broken Red Polished Punctured ware bowls (Ft. 4). The sherds included a preponderance of Red Polished III Mottled ware, small quantities of undecorated Red Polished Punctured ware, and Blue Core ware of a less developed type than that associated with Area A. (The term Red Polished Punctured ware is used here for the first time and is defined below in the discussion of the pottery from Area A.) A negligible amount of Red Polished IV ware and the absence of Proto-white Slip ware lead to the conclusion that Area G was settled during the Middle Bronze Age, and is probably contemporary with some of the tombs in Areas C and J, but earlier than the Late Cypriote IA settlement in Area A.

In the Area C necropolis (Figure 3-3), six intact tombs were excavated by the Kent State University Expedition in 1975 and 1976. Several others had been disturbed by looters, including Tomb 24 b, which still contained 26 vases and a limestone whetstone. The dromoi and tomb chambers were cut out of the *havara* bedrock, and the entrances to the chambers were closed by *plakas*. Several tombs had multiple burials ranging in date from perhaps as early as Early Cypriote III to the beginning of the Middle Cypriote III period. The Early Cypriote III date is based on the presence in Tomb 24 b of Red Polished I South Coast ware, although it seems likely that this ware may have continued in use into the Middle Cypriote period (Swiny 1979: 225). Red Polished IV ware in Tomb 23 d indicates a Middle Cypriote III date for the latest burials, since that ware appears in the Middle Cypriote III period (Karageorghis 1965b: 47).

Tomb 23 d, on the south side of Dromos 23, was intact; its *plaka* was in situ. It contained two chambers. Figure 3-4 shows a north-south section through some of the excavated tombs, including the larger chamber of 23 d. The chamber, like others in the necropolis, has suffered from repeated flooding which had moved the skeletal remains and pottery vases from their original positions. The fragmentary skeletal remains indicated that there had been two burials in the chamber. Of the 12 pottery vases found in the tomb, ten are of Red Polished III Mottled ware, consisting of utilitarian shapes such as bowls, jugs, juglets, and coarse cooking pots, some with incised or relief decoration. Of the two remaining vessels, one is a Red

Polished III black-topped bottle with incised decoration (Figure 3-5), which Herscher (Herscher 1978: 811, note 5) believes was produced at Lapithos in Early Cypriote IIIB/Middle Cypriote I. The other vessel is a Red Polished IV jar with incised decoration (Figure 3-6), which should date from Middle Cypriote III (Karageorghis 1965b: 47). Since Red Polished III Mottled ware appears to have been used extensively in the Middle Cypriote period, it is the least helpful chronologically. Thus, it would seem that the earliest burial in this chamber may be as early as Middle Cypriote I and that the second burial could be as late as Middle Cypriote III. The other finds from this chamber include a copper needle and a necklace of 395 tiny beads (2.5 to 3.0 mm. in diameter) of red and black quartz and white calcite.

The second chamber of Tomb 23 d contained a single burial, eight pottery vases, and a necklace with approximately 500 beads similar to those mentioned above. Seven of the vases are of Red Polished III Mottled ware of shapes similar to those found in the main chamber. The remaining vase is a Red Polished IV coarse storage jar. On the basis of the latter, it would appear that this burial is contemporary with the later burial in the main chamber, i.e., Middle Cypriote III.

It is worth emphasizing that none of the tombs excavated in the necropolis at Phaneromeni, either by the author or by Weinberg, are contemporary with the Late Cypriote IA settlement in Area A.

Although the architectural remains in Area A are rather poorly preserved, having been disturbed by centuries of ploughing and erosion, they are the most extensive of their period to have been excavated thus far in Cyprus. The excavated area (Figure 3-7) contains two architectural complexes with a road passing between them. Each complex consists of multiple, irregularly shaped rooms and courtyards. The walls were constructed with lower courses of riverstones and a few *havara* blocks for their facings, and fragments of *havara* and pebbles, bonded with mud, for their central core. The average thickness of the walls is 0.60 to 0.70 m. Usually only the lowest one or two courses of the walls are preserved, but the western wall of Room 3 has four courses preserved to a height of 0.76 m. The superstructure of the walls was built of mud brick. A few accidentally fired brick fragments indicate that the size of the bricks was approximately 0.10 m. wide by 0.07 m. thick, but their length remains unknown. Foundation trenches were not used, and the walls merely rested on red sandy soil, which also formed the habitation surface of the structures. There were only a few instances where fragments of floors, consisting of compact debris, could be ascertained.

The settlement extended over the area of the dirt road on the south and under the vineyard to the west where further excavations could not be undertaken, but the approximate eastern and northern boundaries of the settlement have been determined.

The plan of Area A (Figure 3-8) indicates the location of other features, such as stone slabs with circular depressions which served as post supports for wooden posts supporting the roofs. Examples of these were found in Rooms 2, 7, 8, 10, 16, and 28. Interior buttresses (?) seem to have been used in Rooms 2 and 28 in conjunction with posts to support ceiling beams. Rooms 10, 14, 18, 19, 28, and 29 were furnished with stone benches of varying width and height constructed against the interior walls. Rectangular hearths were used in Rooms 17 and 30, while circular hearths were found in Rooms 8, 13, 25, and 29. Due to the poor state of preservation of the walls, only six doorways could be identified with certainty and only one pivot stone, not in situ, was found in Room 10, though they were in common use at Middle Cypriote sites such as Dhali-Kafkallia (Overbeck and Swiny 1972: 28).

Another common feature is the existence of lime plaster bins, analyzed by geologist John Gifford. Thrity-four such features are distributed throughout the settlement. Three bins are reinforced at the base with small riverstones, ten are built on stone mortars, nine are on flat slabs of stone exhibiting no wear, two are on large convex river pebbles, and seven have carefully rounded bases without any stone reinforcement. The plaster in the bins is often several layers thick and sometimes slightly fired. The inner diameter at the base of the bins varies from 0.11 to 0.23 m., and the average angle of the sides is between 25 and 30 degrees. Their height is not usually preserved, but Bin 20 in Room 13 is 0.28 m. high with an upper diameter of 0.44 m., and Bin 7 in Room 2 is 0.14 m. high with a diameter of 0.36 m. at the rim. Since the bins were full of occupational debris indistinguishable from that surrounding them, and since their positions provide no clue as to their use, their function remains undetermined.

Five pits, varying from 0.20 to 0.70 m. in diameter, were found in Room 3. They were unlined and their contents did not indicate their use.

The architectural remains in Area A are of one period, although some evidence of minor alterations was discovered, especially in Rooms 8 and 9 where the partition wall between them was constructed later than the adjoining walls. Furthermore, doorways between Rooms 19 and 30, 16 and 18, and 11 and 22 were blocked subsequent to their original construction.

Evidence of collapsed walls, smashed pottery, and deposits of ash provide clear evidence that the settlement was destroyed by fire. Widely scattered sherds from the same vessels, even between different rooms; the discovery of burned and unburned sherds from the same vessel, implying their breakage prior to the fire; and the scarcity of metal objects has led to the conclusion that extensive looting and disturbance occurred before the fire.

Since very little architecture dating from phases of the Cypriote Bronze Age prior to the Late Cypriote II period has been excavated, it is possible to discuss parallels with the architectural remains at Phaneromeni only in a general manner. Some basic resemblances in plan and construction methods between Phaneromeni and other Bronze Age sites can only be pointed out, bearing in mind that until quite recently there had been little change in construction methods and materials used in Cypriote domestic architecture from the Bronze Age to modern times.

No other Bronze Age architecture has yet been excavated in Cyprus contemporary with that in Area A at Phaneromeni. The closest in date are the remains of a private house excavated by Dikaios at Enkomi-Ayios Iakovos (Dikaios 1969a: 155ff.; 1969b: pls. 267-269). The house is dated to the Late Cypriote I period, but later than the remains at Phaneromeni. The materials and methods of construction are similar to Phaneromeni, as are the sizes of rooms and thicknesses of walls.

The small house excavated by Gjerstad at Alambra (Gjerstad 1926: 20-27; Stewart 1962: 215), although much earlier, provides some parallels with Phaneromeni. The room sizes and wall thicknesses are identical. The use of clay benches along interior walls is similar to the stone ones at Phaneromeni, and a slaked lime hearth in one of the rooms is similar in construction to the plaster lined bins at Phaneromeni, though no parallel in shape or use is implied.

At Alambra-Mouttes Area A, the Cornell University excavations (Coleman 1977: 71-79; 1979: 159-167) are providing new information concerning Middle Cypriote architecture. The rectilinear rooms and the regularity of wall construction are more uniform than at Phaneromeni, though the scale of the settlement and the size of the rooms, as well as the use of a bench, are comparable.

Dikaios excavated an industrial smelting complex at Ambelikou-Choma tis Galinis (Dikaios 1946: 244-245; Buchholz and Karageorghis 1973: 132, fig. 53) which he dated to the Early Cypriote period, but Swiny, after studying some of the excavation's pottery now in the Cyprus Museum, suggests a Middle Cypriote date (Swiny 1979: 60). The plan of the ten rooms belonging to this complex suggests a certain lack of architectural cohesion, with irregularly shaped rooms and meandering walls, which compares well with Phaneromeni. The Ambelikou remains, however, do not represent a habitation settlement and some rooms were probably not roofed.

The Middle Cypriote III house at Kalopsidha (Gjerstad 1926: 27-37; Åström 1966: 9-12; 1972a: 1) is probably the best preserved example of Middle Cypriote architecture to have been excavated. Enough artifacts were found in situ in the rooms to allow the proposal of functional attributions for the various rooms. The use of a bench along an interior wall and the scale and form of the rooms are comparable to Phaneromeni, though the thickness of the walls is greater at the latter site. The pluristic function of rooms 9 through 11 at Kalopsidha is parallel to that of most rooms at Phaneromeni. At Phaneromeni, only three rooms can be tentatively identified as having had definite uses based on the artifacts found in them: Room 14, weaving and spinning; Room 28, storage and grinding (food preparation); and Room 16, cooking and grinding.

The Middle Cypriote III house plans at Dhali-Kafkallia (Overbeck and Swiny 1972: 25-28) are not well enough preserved to allow meaningful comparisons with Phaneromeni, except for materials and methods of construction.

In conclusion, from the available evidence it would seem that the most striking feature of Cypriote Bronze Age architecture is its agglutinative nature. Rambling multiroomed complexes arranged around courtyards in which humans and animals lived in close proximity, much as in traditional village houses in Cyprus today, were the norm. Methods and materials of construction seem to have been standard throughout the island, as were such features as interior benches, upright wooden supports, and circular and rectangular hearths.

Artifacts from the occupational debris within the settlement include a surprising number of lithics, especially ground and chipped stone tools. The majority of the ground stone tools are handstones, mortars, and querns. Also included are two types of axes, adze-chisels, tethering stones, and serpentine jewelry. Swiny (1979: 69-138) has developed a typology for the ground stone assemblage from Phaneromeni which is already being used at other excavations of Bronze Age sites in Cyprus. Large quantities of flint tools and debitage were collected from Area A and are being studied by Holly Morris.

In addition, two types of gamestones were found in Area A. Swiny suggests they are related to the Egyptian games of Senet and Mehen (Swiny 1976:43-56; 1980: in press). The Senets (Figure 3-9) contain three rows of ten small depressions each, sometimes with larger depressions on the sides. Not all the examples shown in Figure 3-9 were discovered in situ; many were surface finds from Phaneromeni. The examples of Mehen (Figure 3-10), with an irregular number of depressions arranged in a spiral pattern, are from both stratified contexts and the surface. The large example on the lower right was used as a *plaka* for Tomb 23 e in Area C. Four of the examples are bifacial gamestones with Mehen on one side and Senet on the other. This is a strong argument, along with the portable size of most of the examples, for labelling them gaming stones.

Additional examples of both games were found by Swiny at other Bronze Age sites in southern Cyprus during an intensive surface survey he conducted as part of the Kent State University project in 1978. Senets have also been found at many Bronze Age sites in other parts of Cyprus, but examples of Mehen are rare outside the Episkopi area.

Examples of metal work discovered in Area A include a few needles, awls, tacks, a piece of sheet metal, two arsenical copper knives, and the butt of a third knife. All have been analyzed by Dr. Paul Craddock of the British Museum, and it is important to note that none contain tin. Figure 3-11 shows one of the complete knives. At its widest point the sinuous ogival butt has two rivets with which it was hafted to a wooden (?) handle. It belongs to Åström's Type 2b (Åström 1972a: 139) or Stewart's Type A IVa (Stewart 1962: 350). A larger blade of the same type was found in Tomb I at Pendaiya (Karageorghis 1965b: 81, fig. 13, and Herscher 1976: 13) dated to Late Cypriote IA.

The only evidence for metalworking at Phaneromeni consists of two fragments of a terracotta crucible with prills of arsenical copper still adhering to its inner surface. No slag was found in Area A, so evidence exists only of secondary smelting or repairwork being carried out here.

The terracotta objects from Area A include 58 spherical or roughly biconical spindle whorls with incised decoration, a few conical loom weights, a few beads, and one fragment of a plank-shaped figurine, rare in southern Cyprus.

The settlement in Area A is dated on the basis of the types of non-local pottery, such as White Painted wares and especially Proto-white Slip ware. The White Painted wares include a fragment of a White Painted V juglet (Figure 3-12). Although Proto-white Slip ware comprises only 0.29 percent of the total stratified sherd sample, its presence provides the most accurate indicator of all the wares for the dating of the destruction of the settlement in Area A to the Late Cypriote IA period (Karageorghis 1965b: 55; Merrillees 1971: 60). Figure 3-13 shows an example of a Proto-white Slip quadruped vase.

Red Polished IV ware comprises 35 percent of all sherds recovered from Area A. It was used primarily for closed vessels such as jugs, juglets, and jars/amphorae. Among the unusual shapes are a spouted jug with incised decoration and a unique strainer jug with relief decoration and a peculiar opening in its side (Figure 3-14).

A variety of fine Red Polished ware, often, but not invariably, decorated with incised and punctured decoration, was first discovered in a stratified context at Phaneromeni (Herscher 1976: 11-19). It seems to have been produced locally and in the past has sometimes been called "Episkopi ware" (Tatton-Brown 1979: 35-36). On the basis of the diagnostic decorative style of some of its vessels, it is proposed to rename it "Red Polished Punctured ware," a term offered initially by Swiny (1979: 232-234) in his unpublished doctoral dissertation. It should be emphasized that not all of this ware is decorated; it comes in a plain variety as well. When decorated, however, it displays primarily meticulously incised hook and key patterns, lozenges, and triangles filled with punctures or hatches. The pottery has a well-levigated, fairly soft grit, and fine organic-tempered fabric fired at a low temperature and inconsistently oxidized. Fabric color ranges from buff to dark brown, but when oxidized it is generally light orange. The thin to medium thick slip is carefully burnished to a characteristically smooth, soapy texture, often with visible burnish marks.

Red Polished Punctured ware comprises 37 percent of the total ceramic assemblage in Area A. The undecorated variety was used especially for open shapes, such as small hemispherical bowls. The decorated variety was used for amphorae (Figure 3-15), juglets (Figure 3-16), bowls, and askoi in the shape of stylized birds or with other theriomorphic decoration (Figure 3-17).

Another distinctive type of pottery from Area A is Blue Core ware, which was first recognized by Herscher (1976: 11-19). The fine, hard, grit-tempered fabric was fired at a high temperature for a short time. The core is usually a blue-grey color with only the surface oxidized. The surface is usually pockmarked and sometimes slipped and/or burnished. The surface color ranges from buff to red-brown. It is sometimes decorated with relief and incised designs. Blue Core ware comprises 8.4 percent of the ceramic assemblage from Area A. Closed shapes such as bottles and small amphorae predominate, and most of the storage vessels from Area A were made of a coarse variety of this ware (Figure 3-18).

The faunal remains collected from Area A have been studied by John Watson of The Institute of Archaeology, London, and by Günther Nobis, Bonn. They consist primarily of bones of *bos, sus, ovis, caprovis,* and *Dama Mesopotamica.*

The botanical remains recovered by flotation from Area A are somewhat disappointing. Sixty-two samples, measuring a minimum of 2 litres each, were processed and analyzed by Julie Hansen, the expedition's palaeobotanist. They contained only a few lentil seeds, grape seeds, and an apple or pear seed from Rooms 3, 10, and 28. Cereals were lacking in the samples from Area A, but barley was recovered from the Middle Cypriote tombs in Area C.

From the material remains excavated in Area A, one can reconstruct a self-sufficient community of farmers who cultivated the nearby fields, attended to the needs of their animals, processed their food, produced most of their own pottery and stone and metal implements, and wove the materials for their clothing. They supplemented their diet by hunting and perhaps by fishing and had leisure to play Senet and Mehen. Their limited contacts with other parts of the island are shown by the non-local pottery, especially painted wares; by their use of copper; and perhaps by the games. There is no evidence of foreign contacts.

The lack of fortifications for the settlement seems to indicate a peaceful existence. It is impossible to determine whether the destruction of the settlement was accidental or the result of an altercation. The settlement in Area A lasted for only a few generations. Once it was destroyed the survivors seem to have moved to the site of Bamboula, located on higher ground approximately 500 m. to the northwest. Their ancestors had lived in Area G. One major problem remaining unsolved is where the inhabitants of Area A buried their dead. Perhaps it was within the area of the modern village of Episkopi, but the precise location remains to be determined.

As part of the project during the summer of 1978, Swiny and other staff members undertook a surface reconnaissance of Bronze Age sites in an area of southern Cyprus stretching from the Kouris River westward to the area of Evdhimou and Anoyira villages (Swiny 1979: 240-335; 1981). This survey resulted in the discovery of five previously unrecorded sites, as well as a more complete study of 13 additional sites which had been known before in varying degrees, but most of which had never been published. As a result of the survey, as well as through the excavation of Phaneromeni itself, it is now known that southern Cyprus was much more extensively occupied during the Bronze Age, especially the Middle Bronze Age, than was previously thought (Catling 1962: 129-169).

Some major contributions of this work to the study of Cypriote Bronze Age archaeology can now be summarized. Although the architecture at Phaneromeni shows no evidence of foreign influence, it is comparable both in technique and plan to other sites in Cyprus. The use of stone, mud brick, and wood, as well as irregularly shaped units forming rambling multiroomed complexes, seems to be a standard feature of pre-Late Bronze Age architecture throughout the island.

Among the surprising and most notable results of the excavations are the large quantities of ground and chipped stone implements and the absence of tin bronze implements. The typologies for ground stone implements developed by Swiny, (1979: 69-138) on the basis of the stratified material from Phaneromeni are already being used at other excavations in Cyprus.

Although problems with chronological and stylistic aspects of Cypriote Bronze Age pottery typologies still persist, the ceramic material from stratified contexts at Phaneromeni has significantly contributed to the clarification of some of them, especially regarding regional variations of pottery in southern Cyprus. Further contributions in this regard can be expected when Ellen Herscher completes her study of the pottery from Phaneromeni.

At the very least, the excavations at Phaneromeni and the regional survey have provided a more balanced view of southern Cyprus before the Late Cypriote II period.

ACKNOWLEDGMENTS

The excavations I directed were sponsored by Kent State University, the National Endowment for the Humanities, The Cleveland Foundation Resources, and private individuals.

I wish to express my thanks to Dr. Karageorghis for inviting me to undertake a more extensive excavation of the site of Phaneromeni and for valuable assistance and encouragement over the years, to Dr. Weinberg for making the records of his excavation available to me, and to all the members of my staff especially to my assistant director, Dr. Swiny; Dr. Herscher, our pottery expert; and Lucy MacLaurin. Without the dedicated assistance of my staff and the funding provided by the sources mentioned, this project would not have been possible.

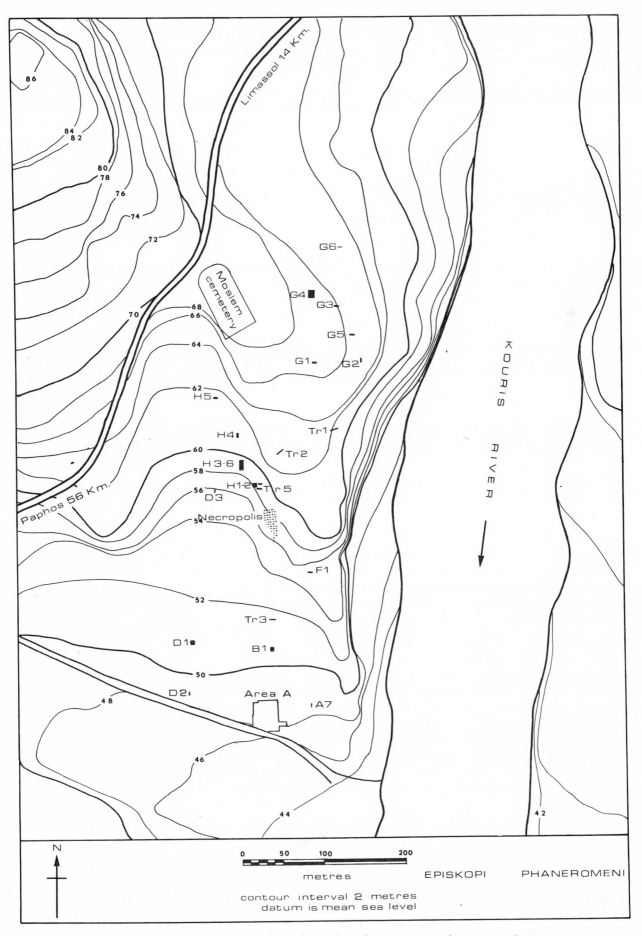

3-1. Contour map of the site showing excavation trenches.

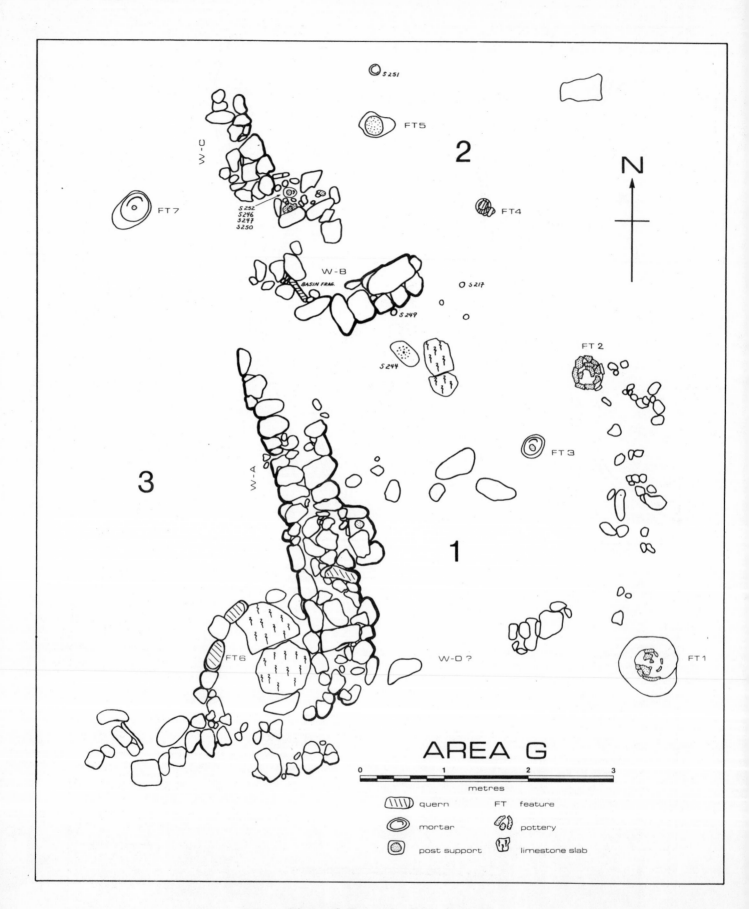

3-2. Plan of Trench G4, Area G.

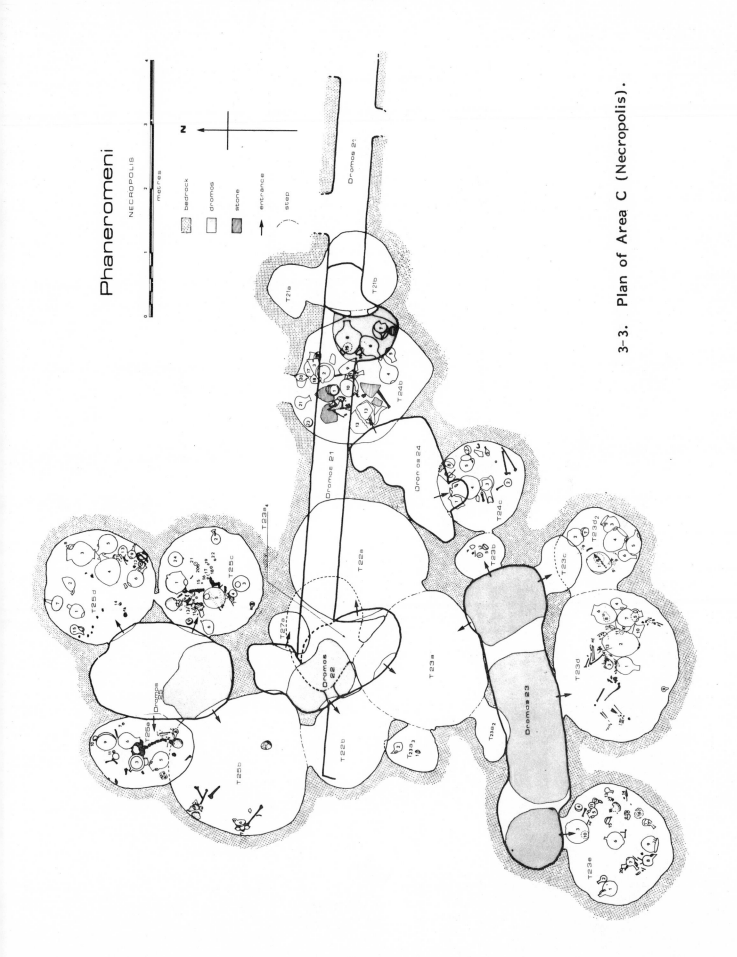

3-3. Plan of Area C (Necropolis).

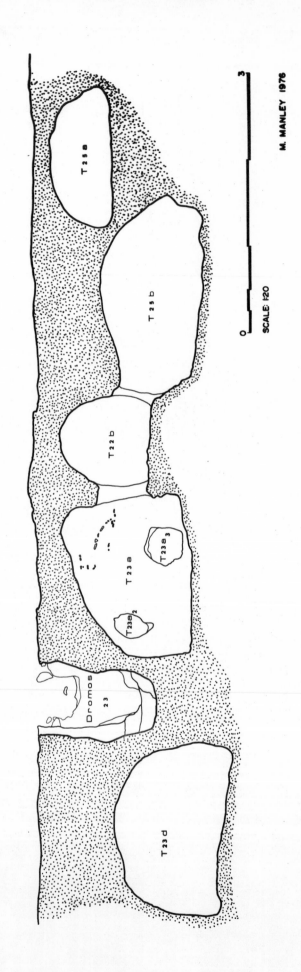

3-4. Section of tombs in Area C (Necropolis).

3-5.   Red Polished III black-topped bottle from Tomb 23 d (Ph/P46).   Photo by Robert K. Vincent, Jr.

3-6.   Red Polished IV jar from Tomb 23 d (Ph/P39). Photo by Robert K. Vincent, Jr.

3-7.   Aerial view of Area A (courtesy RAF Helicopters, Episkopi).

3-8. **Plan of Area A.**

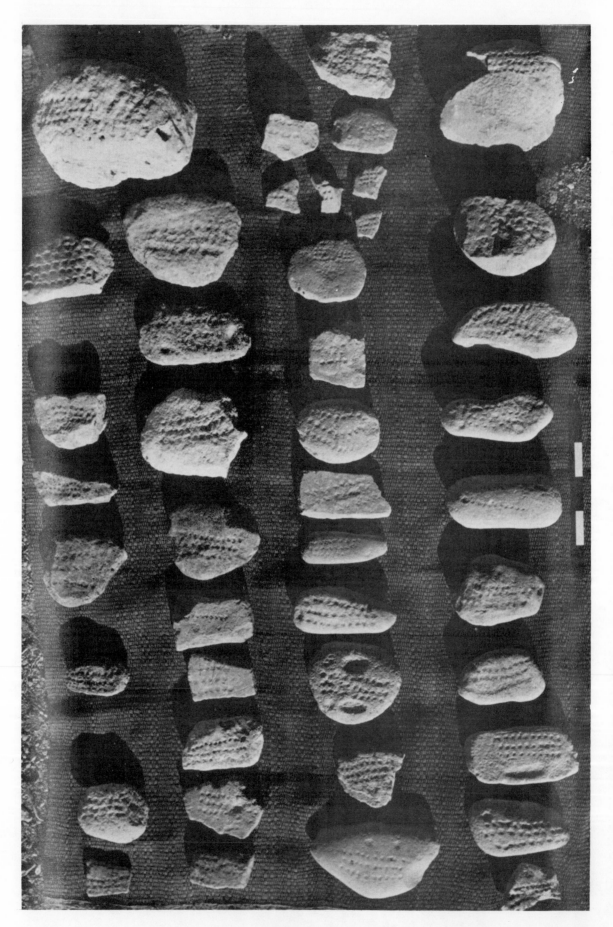

3-9. Gamestones related to the Egyptian game of Senet. Photo by Robert K. Vincent, Jr.

3-10. Gamestones related to the Egyptian game of Mehen. Photo by Robert K. Vincent, Jr.

3-11. Arsenical copper knife from Area A (Ph/M34). Photo by Robert K. Vincent, Jr.

3-12. White Painted V juglet (Ph/P131). Photo by Robert K. Vincent, Jr.

3-13. Proto-white Slip quadruped vase from Area A (Ph/P176). Photo by Robert K. Vincent, Jr.

3-14. Red Polished IV strainer jug from Area A (Ph/P208). Photo by Robert K. Vincent, Jr.

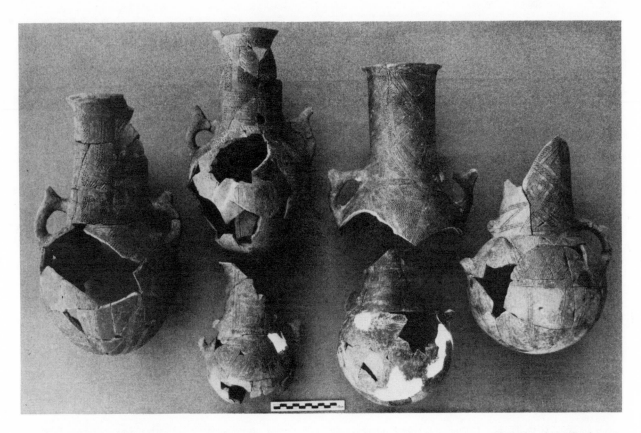

3-15. Red Polished Punctured ware amphorae from Area A. Photo by Robert
K. Vincent, Jr.

3-16. Red Polished Punctured ware juglets from Area A. Photo by Robert K.
Vincent, Jr.

3-17. Red Polished Punctured ware askoi from Area A. Photo by Robert K. Vincent, Jr.

3-18. Blue Core ware pithos from Area A (Ph/P199). Photo by Robert K. Vincent, Jr.

CHAPTER 4.

SOUTHERN CYPRUS, THE DISAPPEARING EARLY BRONZE AGE,

AND THE EVIDENCE FROM PHANEROMENI

Ellen Herscher

It is also necessary to make it clear that
the dating of many sites has become dubious,
since the old equation of Red Polished pottery
with the Early Cypriote period is no longer
valid (Stewart 1962:211).

The development of Cypriote pottery was first characterized by Sir John Myres and presented in detail in 1914 in his *Handbook of the Cesnola Collection*.[1] His scheme, which forms the basis of the standard system of classification still in general use, defined Cypriote cultural phases in terms of the prevailing pottery types ("wares"); wares themselves were distinguished for the most part according to surface treatment. Thus, for the period of the Bronze Age, Red Polished ware was considered the indicator of the Early Cypriote phase, White Painted ware of Middle Cypriote, and Base-ring and White Slip wares of Late Cypriote.

This scheme was refined by Gjerstad's excavations in the 1920s and the Swedish Cyprus Expedition in the 1930s. Studies of this new material revised the definitions of the various periods, which were now considered to be marked by the appearance of the new ware types; however, it was clearly recognized that the earlier wares often persisted into the new phase (Stewart 1962:210, 272-273; Åström 1957:172,274). The site of Lapithos-Vrysi tou Barba on the north coast provided the bulk of material, consisting of the contents of 23 tombs, used in the formulation of the Early and Middle Cypriote periods. Seriation of the pottery from these tombs built the chronological framework, which continued to maintain that White Painted ware was the indicator of the Middle Cypriote period (in spite of Stewart's caveat which began this paper).

These were the principles Catling used to identify sites in his important 1955-1959 survey work. In 1962 he presented his results in what was to become the accepted view of Cypriote settlement patterns in the Bronze Age (Catling 1962:129-169).

Perhaps Catling's most puzzling conclusion was the apparent depopulation of southern and western Cyprus in Middle Cypriote, based on the observed lack of White Painted ware in the area. This region appeared to be heavily settled in both the Early and Late Cypriote periods (and indeed in all other periods of Cypriote history and pre-history), conditions which made this supposed gap all the more difficult to explain (Catling 1962:139). A more recent survey produced similar results (Adovasio, Fry, Gunn, and Maslowski 1974: 345-347).

In the meantime, an Early Bronze Age settlement had become the Holy Grail of Cypriote archaeology as further work on the period, for example at Vounous, continued to uncover only tombs (Stewart and Stewart 1950).[2] A settlement site at Episkopi-Phaneromeni had been identified as Early Cypriote on the basis of the Red Polished ware found on the surface (Catling 1962:150). Therefore, Professor Saul Weinberg conducted excavations there in 1955 for the University of Missouri (Weinberg 1956:112-121). Red Polished ware was found in quantity, and, although the distinct character of the material was noted (Duryea 1965:73), the limited nature of the soundings precluded any final conclusions regarding the site's significance. In 1975 investigations at Phaneromeni were resumed by Kent State University under the direction of James R. Carpenter; the results of the four Kent State seasons to date have made it possible to revise fundamentally the accepted view of the Cypriote Bronze Age by demonstrating the distinct regional nature of the area, characterized by the failure to adopt White Painted ware for local manufacture in the Middle Cypriote period.

That considerable regional variation existed in the pottery of Cyprus in the Early and Middle Bronze Age is not a new idea; it was recognized by James Stewart and has been noted by several other scholars (Karageorghis 1940-48:117; Herscher 1973:62,69-70; 1976:11-15; Merrillees 1978:26-28; Frankel 1974:10-11 and note 140 for additional references). In fact, it became apparent in recent years that there are other parts of Cyprus which did not produce White Painted ware, at least in the earlier stages of Middle Cypriote, such as the Karpas (see, for example Herscher 1973:62-71). However, the excavations at Phaneromeni provided the necessary cross-links -- in the form of stratified "imports" from northern parts of the island -- to closely date the south coast style as represented there.[3] Thus, in spite of the predominance of Red Polished ware, it is now clear that the Phaneromeni cemetery dates to Middle Cypriote and the settlement to Late Cypriote IA; furthermore, the varieties of pottery previously thought to be all "Red Polished ware" in fact do demonstrate a sequence of development.

Obviously, at Phaneromeni it has not been possible to classify the local pottery on the primary basis of surface treatment as had been the tradition in Cypriote archaeology: in those terms, most of it still remains Red Polished ware (cf. Merrillees 1978:26-27). However, it has been possible to distinguish a sequence of development based on analysis of fabric and method of manufacture, which also reveals the progress of ceramic technology in the area.

The five (probably) local fabrics which have been distinguished are:

1. Red Polished I - South Coast (Figure 4-1) (Stewart 1962:270,359, figs. LXXIII. 1-3, CVII. 1-2, CXLII. 19-20): a fine, soft, thick-walled fabric, with grit and organic temper, unevenly slipped, often incompletely oxidized, usually lustrous, and perhaps made only for funerary use

2. Red Polished III Mottled (Figure 4-2): a hard, fairly coarse, grit-tempered

fabric with slightly lustrous slip

3.   Red Polished Punctured ware (Figure 4-3): a finer, light brown grit and organic-tempered fabric, slipped and often with fine punctured decoration

4.   Red Polished IV (Figure 4-4): a very hard, thin-walled, dark brown, grit-tempered fabric, apparently unslipped, which appears to evolve into Late Cypriote Monochrome ware

5.   Blue Core ware (Figure 4-5): of which Drab Polished ware is a variation and which appears to evolve into Late Cypriote Base-ring ware; a fine, hard fabric tempered with abundant limestone inclusions, oxidized only on the surface, sometimes thinly slipped

Each of these five fabrics varies considerably in surface color, often on the same vessel.

In view of these revisions and the discovery that most Red Polished ware in southern Cyprus dates to the Middle Cypriote period, the question now arises whether there is any Early Cypriote culture in the south. Was the area depopulated at this time, rather than in Middle Cypriote, as previously thought?

In 1978 Stuart Swiny conducted survey work in the area (Swiny 1979) which included the reexamination of the sites recorded as Early Cypriote by Catling and Dikaios (1962:148-154). Swiny found pottery comparable to that from Phaneromeni, but none that definitely can be attributed to the Early Bronze Age. He also located several promising habitation sites which warrant more thorough examination. Certainly only further excavation, preferably of a stratified site, can resolve the remaining problems with any degree of certainty.

However, the richness of both the Chalcolithic (Karageorghis 1973a:635-638; 1977:740; Peltenburg 1977:140-143) and the Middle Cypriote in southwestern Cyprus would seem to argue against any intervening depopulation in the region. A more reasonable hypothesis suggests that regional distinction is present in the earlier periods as well, with the highly developed Chalcolithic cultures continuing in the south well after the new Early Bronze Age features had been established in the north; in fact, the Chalcolithic may have continued as late as a time contemporary with Early Cypriote III elsewhere (for a hypothetical reconstruction, see Figure 4-6). At present, the beginnings of the Early Bronze Age in Cyprus are poorly known and little understood (Dikaios 1962:190-191; Stewart 1962:210-211, 269-271; Merrillees 1966:33-35; Catling 1971:808-813), but they do seem to be focused in the north or the Ovgos Valley, from which areas the culture may have spread slowly, reaching the south and west toward the close of the period.

In spite of the eventual arrival of Early Cypriote features (e.g., beak-spouted jugs, hook-tanged daggers, and rock-cut chamber tombs) in the south and west, extreme regionalism continued throughout the island during Middle Cypriote and into Late Cypriote IA. The late years of this interval are marked by the construction of fortifications at several sites; Late Cypriote IA was brought to an end by destructions, at least in a few cases, as for example at Kalopsidha and Phaneromeni (cf. Merrillees 1971:56-79; Åström 1972d:46-57). The evidence is still scanty, but it at least suggests the possibility that political divisions accompanied the cultural ones apparent in the archaeological record. Whatever the cause or causes, Late Cypriote IB brings striking changes: relocation of settlements, the appearance of writing and imported Aegean pottery, and, perhaps most revealing, a homogeneous culture throughout Cyprus.

Certainly these events signal an end to the island's long isolation, and it is quite possible that copper played some role in such a radical change.[4] There is no firm evidence for actual smelting of copper in Cyprus before this time, and it coincides with increased metal needs elsewhere, particularly in the Aegean. As is so well documented in later periods of the history of Cyprus, it appears that even at this early date external forces may have drastically shaped the form of Cypriote culture.

NOTES

1. *For a more detailed discussion of the background of Cypriote pottery classification, see Frankel (1974: 1-3), Merrillees (1978: chapter II).*

2. *Gjerstad's house at Alambra (1926:19-27) would today be dated to Middle Cypriote I since it contained White Painted ware from its first period of occupation (ibid.:26; cf. Stewart 1962:215).*

3. *They also confirm the revised dating of the Kalavasos tombs originally published by Karageorghis (1940-48:116-141). See Herscher (1976:13) and Todd et al. (1978: 191-193; 1979b:283-284).*

4. *Merrillees (1971:77-78) had suggested general commercial causes.*

4-1. Red Polished I ware -
South Coast (Ph/P61). Photo
by Robert K. Vincent, Jr.

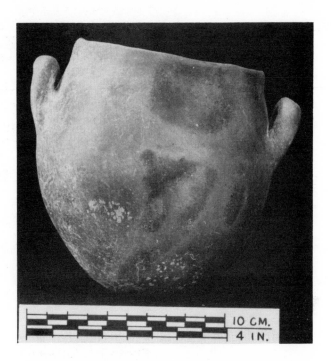

4-2. Red Polished III Mottled ware,
(Ph/P10). Photo by Robert K. Vincent, Jr.

4-3. Red Polished Punctured ware
(Ph/P164). Photo by Robert K.
Vincent, Jr.

4-4. Red Polished IV ware (Ph/P220).
Photo by Robert K. Vincent, Jr.

4-5. Blue Core ware (Ph/P68).
Photo by Robert K. Vincent, Jr.

HYPOTHETICAL RECONSTRUCTION OF REGIONAL CHRONOLOGIES

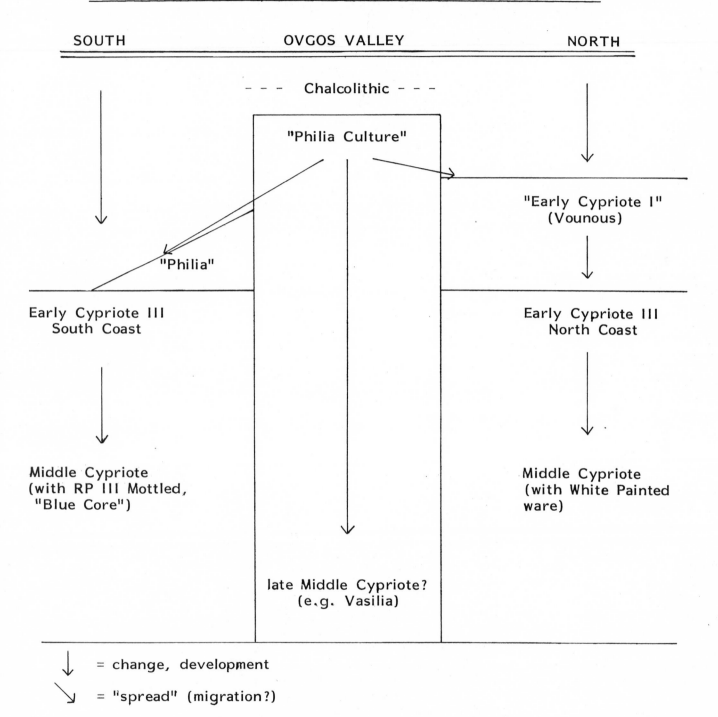

4-6.   Hypothetical reconstruction of regional chronologies.

Part III

Paphos Region

CHAPTER 5.

RECENT ARCHAEOLOGICAL DISCOVERIES AT KOUKLIA

Vassos Karageorghis

Kouklia, on the west coast of Cyprus, lies on the site of Palaeopaphos, which, according to later Greek authors and to tradition (Strabo 14.6.3), was built by Agapenor, one of the heroes of the Trojan war. After the Trojan War, some of the heroes went to Cyprus where they founded cities. Agapenor, leader of the Arcadians in the Trojan War, built Paphos. Others, Teucer, for instance, built Salamis. Paphos has been the subject of many controversies, and several scholars have excavated in the region of Paphos looking for the Paphos of Agapenor. In the early 1950s, Jean Berard excavated a cemetery in Nea Paphos because he believed that Agapenor's city lay in that area. He found tombs of the 9th and 8th centuries B.C., but nothing earlier. This discovery was not sufficient to justify the suggestion that Nea Paphos was really the site of Agapenor's city.

In 1954 Dr. P. Dikaios excavated a settlement at Palaeokastro, about 4 miles north of Paphos. There he found a military post which he believed might have been one of the first settlements of the Achaeans of Agapenor who later moved inland. Recent excavations carried out by the Swiss-German archaeological mission and also later by the Cypriote Department of Antiquities have now established beyond any doubt that the Paphos of Agapenor is the site of Palaeopaphos, today called Kouklia, where the temple of Aphrodite was. In fact, according to tradition, Agapenor built the temple of Aphrodite and became her first priest.

The site of the recent excavations conducted by the Department of Antiquities from April to August 1979[1] lies about 1 mile southeast of Kouklia. Three tombs were excavated there in the 1950s by a British expedition. During leveling operations there for agricultural works, many tombs were found on the slope of the plateau, 35 of which have so far been excavated. All were intact. The fact that they are about 4 m. below the surface, and that their roofs had collapsed, protected them from looters. The tombs are usually constructed with a long dromos leading to the tomb chamber, and the stomion, or mouth of the chamber, is blocked with stones. Figure 5-1 shows the blocking of one of the tombs and the depth from the surface to the floor of the tomb. Since the roof of this tomb had collapsed, all the material was broken, especially the pottery. Frequently, however, intact vases were found piled one on top of the other. One hundred objects, on the average, were found in each tomb, resulting in about 4,000 objects being recovered during one season's work.

Quite often two burial layers were observed. In one tomb an 11th century burial was covered with about 50 cm. of soil and a 7th century burial placed on top. The inhabitants of Palaeopaphos obviously were interested in their city's past and, in the process of digging foundation trenches for new houses, must have come across objects of earlier periods. In an 8th century tomb, two cylinder seals dating to the 14th and 13th centuries were found lying near the skeleton, and, in an 11th century B.C. tomb, a cache of stone tools dating to the Chalcolithic period was found. At Kouklia an interest in antiquity had, therefore, already started in the 11th century B.C.

The pottery from the tombs is of very good quality. From an 11th century tomb comes a Bichrome jug decorated with schematized birds. This is the beginning of the pictorial style which flourished during the 9th, 8th, and 7th centuries B.C. Also from an 11th century tomb comes a White Painted I kylix with geometric designs derived from the end of the Mycenaean period through the Proto-White Painted style. A kylix with double walls in White Painted I ware is a good example of the Cypriote potter's exuberant style (Figure 5-2). Liquid was poured into the bowl through the mouth of a frog in relief and was poured out through the mouth of a bull protome. Further examples of this exuberant pottery style are two jugs, one in Proto-White Painted ware from the beginning of the 11th century (Figure 5-3), the other in White Painted I style dated to about the middle of the 11th century. Stylistically, they were probably made by the same person. The first has a strainer incorporated into the beard of the head modeled at the top. Askoi of the 11th century are numerous from Palaeopaphos and are represented by a typical one in the form of an animal with a hole through its mouth and a strainer at the tail (Figure 5-4).

A plate of the 11th century presents an interesting scene (Figure 5-5). The base is decorated with a monster in the shape of a two-headed snake. In the field, two figures are depicted trying to kill the monster, one shooting it with a bow and arrow, the other holding what is probably a sword. There are footprints in the field, showing that the scene is taking place in the open air. This scene is very reminiscent of the Greek myth of Herakles and Iolaos killing the Lernaean Hydra, and it is not unlikely that early myths which originated in the Aegean were brought to Cyprus by Achaean settlers, the Mycenaean aristocrats who settled in Paphos.

Many Canaanite jars have been found, showing that the early Achaeans traded with the Near East as their ancestors did. Syro-Palestinian pottery, found in great quantity, is also evidence of trade. Some of the pottery illustrates the origin of Black-on-Red ware. Figure 5-6 shows a lentoid jug decorated with red slip, which has largely worn off, black decoration, and traces of white decoration. The fabric is not Cypriote; thus, this type of pottery must have been introduced from the Syro-Palestinian coast. Another example of an import is an Egyptian faience bowl. The 11th century settlers were following a tradition already begun in the 14th and 15th centuries with the Mycenaean traders.

One of the most interesting finds from the 1979 season is a limestone bathtub. It is 1.50 m. long, 1 m. high, and decorated in relief with designs recalling metal work. A small container on the side must have held herbs or perfume, the soap of the period. Terracotta bathtubs are known from Cyprus, various parts of the Near East, and Greece, but, as far as is known, this is the first time a limestone bathtub has been found. Whether it was placed in the tomb for ritual purposes, or because the deceased wished to have his bathtub with him in the after life, or perhaps just as a symbol of wealth and status is not known. In another tomb, a miniature steatite bathtub was found.

Mycenaean women introduced new fashions into Cyprus. Fibulae of Greek type have been found before in Cyprus in contexts dating to the 11th century. Bronze fibulae were found at Kouklia, and also one, of the D-shape type known from the Aegean, in silver with gold beads. The fibulae from Kouklia are quite large. Bronze pins similar to ones discovered in the Kerameikos in Athens were also found in 11th century tombs.

Bronze tripods were probably numerous at Kouklia. Although only two were found, many examples in terracotta were recovered. Obviously, the bronze tripods were the prototypes for the clay ones. Some bronze tripods may have originated in Cyprus and been exported to Greece and Crete.

A large number of bronze vessels were found. One large bowl, about 30 cm. in diameter, has interesting handles with large stylized lotus flowers at the top and a rectangular plate which joins the handle to the body, somewhat similar to orientaliz-ing bowls of later Etruscan-Orientalizing art. Another large bowl, approximately 40 cm. in diameter, has goat protomes at the top of the handles (Figure 5-7). This is the first time such objects have been found on Cyprus, and it seems most likely that the revival of the art of metallurgy and the subsequent skill in that art were introduced by the Achaeans who settled in Cyprus ca. 1200 B.C. Tripod cauldrons also occur here for the first time, no doubt introduced by the Achaeans since such objects are known from Greece.

The early inhabitants of Kouklia used a Cypriote script, but at the same time a script that was a survival of the Cypro-Minoan script. A bowl, found on the surface during bulldozing, displays signs of the undeciphered Cypro-Minoan script. The tomb in which the bathtub was found also produced three bronze obeloi, or spits, one of which is decorated with engraved signs of the Cypriote syllabary (Figure 5-8). According to Oliver and Emilia Masson, who have seen photographs of the inscription, it should be read as a proper name in Greek, Opheltes, in the genitive case, Opheltau. This type of genitive is characteristic of the Arcadian dia-lect. The inscription dates to the 11th century and is the earliest Greek inscription yet found on Cyprus. The Arcadian dialect is direct proof of the connections be-tween Paphos and Agapenor, the leader of the Arcadians in the Trojan War.

The Mycenaean aristocrats buried at Kouklia in the 11th century were interred with all sorts of weapons. A bronze spearhead and two swords of a type known elsewhere only from tombs in Greece, particularly in the Kerameikos in Athens, are examples.

Quantities of gold were found in the tombs. Gold plaques are decorated with repoussé, and rosettes made from thin gold sheets decorated the garments. Ear-rings also were found. Other gold plaques are decorated in repoussé with a chariot and charioteer, and one with the figure of Astarte in the window. A gold head of Astarte is of a type and subject very common at the end of the Late Bronze Age. A gold needle was found in the tomb of a young girl of about 15 years of age. It was very moving to see that the mother of this young girl lovingly offered her a needle for her needs during the second life.

In the 9th and 8th centuries B.C., life continued at Kouklia in the same exuber-ant style. The tombs of this period produced rich offerings, including quantities of gold objects and good quality pottery. Terracottas were also offered to children as illustrated by horse and rider figurines found in infant graves.

The finds presented here are just a preview of what was found at Kouklia during the summer of 1979. Many more tombs await excavation. With the collaboration of the Swiss-German mission, excavation will continue at this site, which illustrates a very interesting and crucial period in the history of Cyprus, the 11th century. In Greece and elsewhere, this period is called the Dark Ages when poverty reigned. On Cyprus they were not very dark and certainly not poverty stricken.

NOTES

1. *For a more detailed account see Karageorghis (1980).*

5-1. Tomb at Palaeopaphos. Published by permission   of the Director of Antiquities and the Cyprus Museum.

5-2. Kylix with double walls in White Painted I ware. Published by permission of the Director of Antiquities and the Cyprus Museum.

5-3. Jug in Proto-White Painted ware. Published by permission of the Director of Antiquities and the Cyprus Museum.

5-4. Askos in animal form. Published by permission of the Director of Antiquities and the Cyprus Museum.

5-5. Plate in White Painted I ware. Published by permission of the Director of Antiquities and the Cyprus Museum.

5-6. Syro-Palestinian jug with red slip and black and white decoration. Published by permission of the Director of Antiquities and the Cyprus Museum.

5-7. Bronze bowl with goat protome handles. Published by permission of the Director of Antiquities and the Cyprus Museum.

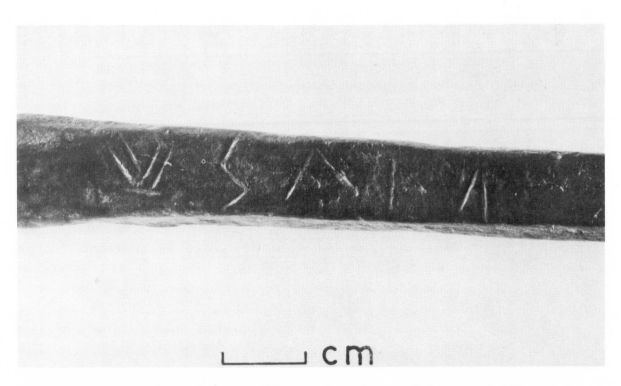

5-8. Bronze spit engraved with the Cypriote syllabary. Published by permission of the Director of Antiquities and the Cyprus Museum.

Part IV

Kourion

CHAPTER 6.

EXCAVATIONS IN THE SANCTUARY OF APOLLO HYLATES

AT KOURION, 1979 AND 1980

Diana Buitron

and

David Soren

The 1979 and 1980 campaigns at the Sanctuary of Apollo Hylates at Kourion were the second and third to be sponsored by the University of Missouri, The Walters Art Gallery, Dartmouth College, and the University of Maryland, Baltimore County. The 1979 season was funded by a matching grant from the National Endowment for the Humanities.

The site is located on the south coast on cliffs overlooking the Bay of Episkopi (Figure 6-1) and was excavated from 1935 to 1953 by a team from the University of Pennsylvania under the direction of George McFadden (1938:10-17; 1940:22-28; 1950: 14-26; 1951:167-168; 1952a:128-129; 1952b:588-590). The new excavations are designed to continue and expand the earlier work.

The sanctuary consists of a half dozen exposed buildings in an area roughly 150 m. square (Figure 6-2). The visitor of antiquity probably entered through one of two gates, either the Kourion Gate at the southeast or the Paphos Gate at the southwest. The weary pilgrim could then spend the night in either the South Building or the Northwest Building, which were probably dormitories. For exercise, there was a palaestra or gymnasium in the Southeast Building; for ablutions, the baths were just to the north. The Archaic Precinct in the northeast part of the sanctuary, named for the numerous terracotta votive figurines of archaic date found there, constituted the sacred heart of the complex. The Precinct contained a large, circular rubble altar, perhaps the one mentioned by Strabo the Geographer (14.6.3) who visited Kourion during the reign of the emperor Augustus (27 B.C. - A.D. 14). Strabo also observed the cliff near the sanctuary from which those who touched and thus defiled the altar of Apollo were flung. Just to the south was the priest's quarters in the East Complex. To the north the Temple of Apollo provided dramatic focus with its extraordinary view over the Bay of Episkopi. A wide paved street leading up to the temple was the principal route for the worshippers, many of whom must have waited in the central court before it was their turn to enter. Along the street a kitchen was located at the south and a stoa or portico just to the north; a semicircular monument stood across from the central court. A peribolos, or boundary wall, encompassed most of the sanctuary's major buildings.

Excavations during the summers of 1979 and 1980 were concentrated in four critical areas: the Archaic Precinct, the Temple of Apollo, the West Enclosure, and the area east of the Southeast Building. All these areas yielded significant results.

ARCHAIC PRECINCT

The circular rubble altar (Figure 6-3 and 6-4) was cleaned of extraneous boulders and debris, thus revealing more clearly its circular shape. Professor Robert Scranton supervised the cleaning and identified the stones he believes are in situ. These stones were then examined by the team's geologist, Dr. Reuben Bullard, who determined that the stones making up the altar came from a quarry different from the one that supplied most of the other sanctuary buildings. The altar was built at a different time and may predate the Roman period of construction.

Rubble altars of this type are apparently not known elsewhere on Cyprus, although circular altars were found at Ayia Irini, but these were smaller and had smooth, hard surfaces (Sjöqvist 1933:308-359). The closest parallels for this kind of rubble altar are in the Near East, for example the altar at Megiddo which is larger and, of course, much older (Yadin 1977:833, 837).

The large worked stone block found lying near the altar (Figure 6-4) was interpreted by Scranton (1967:6-8) as a fence post, one of a series that circled the altar, connected by a wooden beam or rope. This would provide an effective barrier and lends support to Strabo's statement that those who touched the altar of Apollo (if this is the altar in question) were thrown into the sea from the nearby cliffs (Scranton 1967: 9, note 9). Another theory is that it served as a cult stone, and this theory is supported by the fact that only one such stone has been found so far. The concept of a sacred stone with a perforation in which the spirit of the god dwells was discussed by Ohnefalsch-Richter (1893:352) for Paphos. Cult stones for curing fevers exist at Sotira and Episkopi. With these, small children are healed miraculously or virgins may be imbued with potential fertility if they crawl through the hole during a ceremony. The Kourion hole, it must be noted, is too small for such activity.

As the altar was excavated in 1980, two small bulls, one gold and one silver, were found sealed intact within it (Figure 6-5 and 6-6). These magnificient cast objects with separately applied legs are now being studied, but the importance of the bull as a fertility symbol and sign of the return of spring cannot be denied in this cult which even features bull-headed priests in terracotta form.

TEMPLE OF APOLLO

Excavation in trenches Jc and Jd during 1978 (Figure 6-7) had provided pottery evidence for dating the second temple to at least the later 1st or early 2nd century A.D. (Soren 1979:321-327), but the date of the first temple is more difficult to ascertain. In 1979, the interior of the temple, both cella and pronaos, was excavated. The fill contained almost entirely Cypro-Archaic and Cypro-Classical pottery fragments, with a few imported Attic black-figure and red-figure fragments. Traces of the early temple floor were found preserved along the west and south walls of the cella, and traces of the second temple floor, including a depression where a pithos once sat, were found along the east temple wall at a higher level.

Outside the temple, the area to the north was cleaned, revealing blocks of the north wall which had fallen in an earthquake (Figure 6-7 and 6-8). Much of the upper third of the building was lying exactly as it had fallen. One column capital, noted earlier by Scranton (1967:22, note 1), was still lying east of the temple.

Professor Scranton, returning to the Apollo Sanctuary after a 17-year absence, studied the temple in detail, and architectural assistant, Alexandra Corn, working with him, produced the first attempt in 1979 at restoring the temple on paper. But in 1980 architect John Rutherford, assisted by John Huffstot, was able to study every aspect of some 60 blocks lying in the immediate vicinity of the temple.

Rutherford has made a major contribution by overturning the Scranton hypothesis that the surviving architectural fragments came from temples of two different periods. Rutherford showed that the existing remains belonged to a single building, the second temple. This temple is difficult to date, but an inscribed block discovered in 1980 suggests that the second temple will prove to be in fact Neronian.

It was not possible to find examples of every part of the second temple since only the stair, cella crosswall, and podium are in place. But the combined efforts of Scranton and Rutherford, supported by Corn and Huffstot, have turned up evidence for the entire entablature, capitals, and rear pilasters (Figure 6-9, 6-10).

The doorway height of the temple is uncertain and, since no column bases or shafts were found, these parts of the reconstruction are conjectural. However, Professor Loulloupis of the Cypriote Department of Antiquities has excavated an as yet unpublished building at the Kourion city site about 100 m. north of the so-called gymnasium. There, similar capitals were found, dated by Loulloupis to the 2nd century, but featuring volutes which the Temple of Apollo lacked. Professor Loulloupis has generously allowed the authors use of the column shafts and bases from his columns as the basis for the restoration on paper of the temple. The proportions of the shafts and bases were adjusted since the capital is slightly smaller.

We do not know how early the first temple is, but just east of the southern corner of the temple two oval pits, possibly contemporary with it, were found cut into the bedrock. Their purpose remains unclear, as well as their date, but the southernmost was mortared into a bowl-shaped form with a small circular depression in the center (Soren 1979:325). This would appear to provide a base for a pithos or storage jar, and so this area may have contained the sacred stores for the sanctuary. However, no trace of mortar occurs in the second pit. Is the mortaring an adaptive re-use of what was originally a tomb? Are there more pits in this area awaiting excavation? The 1981 season should provide some answers.[1]

Immediately southwest of the temple a curious channel runs under and at a right angle to the structure (Figure 6-2). McFadden found the channel in 1935, but never published it, although he observed in his notes that it was a rock-cut water channel which apparently ran down from the water distribution center at the north end of the sanctuary (McFadden 1935-53:11-17).[2] The exploration of this channel was begun but not completed in 1980. Many local inhabitants consider it to be either an oracular crawlspace or some kind of water system or drain. As the channel turns eastward from the temenos wall of the sanctuary, it bifurcates just a few meters before running under the steps leading up to the temple. The part of the channel which continues eastward stops under the temple steps, while the northeastern branch of the channel also stops after progressing just a short distance.

Obviously, this channel, which predates at least the second temple, could not have carried water anywhere. What was it? One possibility is that it was a planting bed for a line of bushes or trees. The line follows the later temenos wall for some considerable distance and turns at a spot which could have marked the limit of the sanctuary before the first temple. The high bedrock could have necessitated the cutting of the channel for plantings. This suggestion is also strengthened by the fact that yet another channel, which also seems to go nowhere, was discovered (but not published) by McFadden just in front of the Hellenistic East Stoa, a perfect spot for planting (McFadden 1935-53:731).

Another theory has the channels as water troughs for animals, a practice still current in parts of Cyprus. The dates of the channels are not known, but may be among the Hellenistic refinements of the site.

WEST ENCLOSURE

In 1978, square Hg (Figure 6-11) revealed a portion of a curved rubble wall. This wall was investigated in 1979 and 1980 with surprising results. A circular structure or Tholos (Figure 6-11 and 6-12), approximately 18 m. in diameter was uncovered (Buitron and Soren 1979:24-28). The structure consists of a ring-shaped surface made of pebbles set in mortar with a plaster facing that curves slightly downward toward the center of the circle. A rubble foundation for a retaining wall or wide curb surrounds this ring-shaped surface. No trace of a floor exists within the circle, and the curved mortar floor continues down to bedrock, which is quite high in this part of the sanctuary. Seven pits, averaging a little less than a meter in depth and diameter, were cut into bedrock. The authors suggest that the pits represent the location of bushes or sacred trees, perhaps date palms which have root systems that could survive in pits of this size, and that the ring-shaped walkway was for sacred dances or processions. Support for this theory is offered by the existence of numerous Cypriote terracotta groups consisting of figures holding hands around a tree (Ohnefalsch-Richter 1893: pl. LXXVI; Young 1955:220; also see article by Darice Birge within this volume).[3] The rubble foundation suggests that a wall hid the ceremony from public view, but, since the structure is on a man-made terrace, the wall may have served a retaining function as well.

The complete structure was exposed in 1980, with six of the pits forming a roughly circular arrangement just inside the edge of the walkway. One pit, smaller and more shallow than the other six, breaks the line of the circle to the north. This means that either the pit is in an entrance area to the circular structure, or that the pit pre-dates the structure and the ring-shaped surface has not been preserved in this area.

In favor of the north entry theory is the fact that the temenos wall to the north is slightly depressed just opposite the pit and, in fact, contains cuttings for a large doorway.

The circular structure's construction date can be suggested from sherds found in the fill of the terrace on which it sits. Among them was an Arretine rim frag-ment of the early 1st century after Christ, so the final version of the structure should not be earlier than the Julio-Claudian period.

If the interpretation of the features described is correct, then this particular combination of architectural elements with sacred trees is unique. Sacred trees and sacred groves are known elsewhere in Cyprus and are particularly common in the Near East, but so far nothing like this arrangement is associated with them.

EAST OF THE SOUTHEAST BUILDING

In the southeast area of the site was the Southeast Building, a fine palaestra featuring a handsome statue of an athletic Apollo looking out over a large central court. This area flourished until the earthquake of ca. 370 A.D. Following the disaster, a squatter occupation was erected against the eastern area of the building, at first taking the form of a leveling stratum made of caliche, the solution weathering of carbonate bedrock. Several late bronze coins were sealed in the floor, including one of the type of Securitas Rei Publicae with a victory striding left, datable to about the time of the quake, possibly of Valens or Valentinian I.

After this initial floor was installed, a series of walls was added over it and against the now defunct palaestra (Figure 6-13). Much collapsed material left over from the earlier building was mounded up and used as filler (statumen) for a late floor associated with the walls (Figure 6-14). One sherd from among this debris has been dated by John Hayes, author of *Late Roman Pottery*, to at least the very end of the 5th century after Christ, providing some idea for the date of the last major squatter occupation on the site.

CONCLUSION

The discoveries at the sanctuary provided important insights into the urban development of the site, dated several undated structures, brought to light strikingly beautiful objects, led to the total reconstruction of a famous temple, and revealed a tholos apparently unique in Mediterranean archaeology. 1981 should provide even more delights and surprises!

NOTES

1. For dedicatory pithoi at the sanctuary, see Mitford (1971:238-240) and Scranton (1967:25).

2. Scranton (1967:63) discusses the castellum as a "fourth major cistern." See also Last (1975:35,59).

3. This comparison was first suggested to the authors by Vassos Karageorghis.

ACKNOWLEDGMENTS

The staff in 1979 and 1980 consisted of John Rutherford and John Huffstot, Architects; Robert Scranton, Architectural Consultant; Alexandra Corn, Architectural Draftsman; John Huffstot, Photographer and Draftsman; Reuben Bullard and Frank Koucky, Geologists; Terry Weisser, Conservator; Sian Jones, Registrar; Giraud Foster, Osteologist; and Joseph Greene, Field Supervisor. Special thanks to Warrant Officer Harry Heywood and Audrey Heywood.

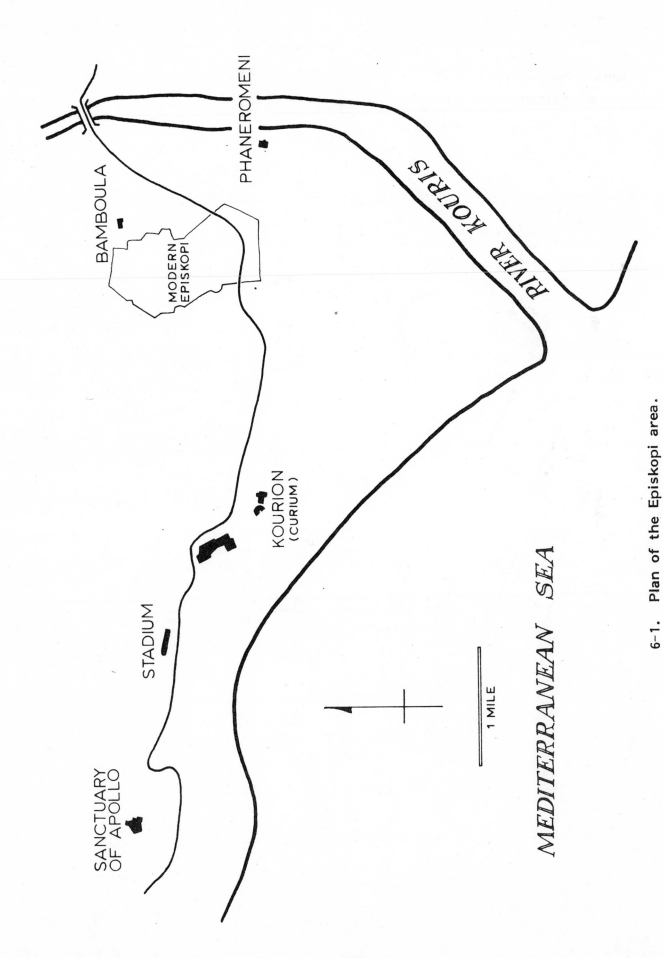

6-1. Plan of the Episkopi area.

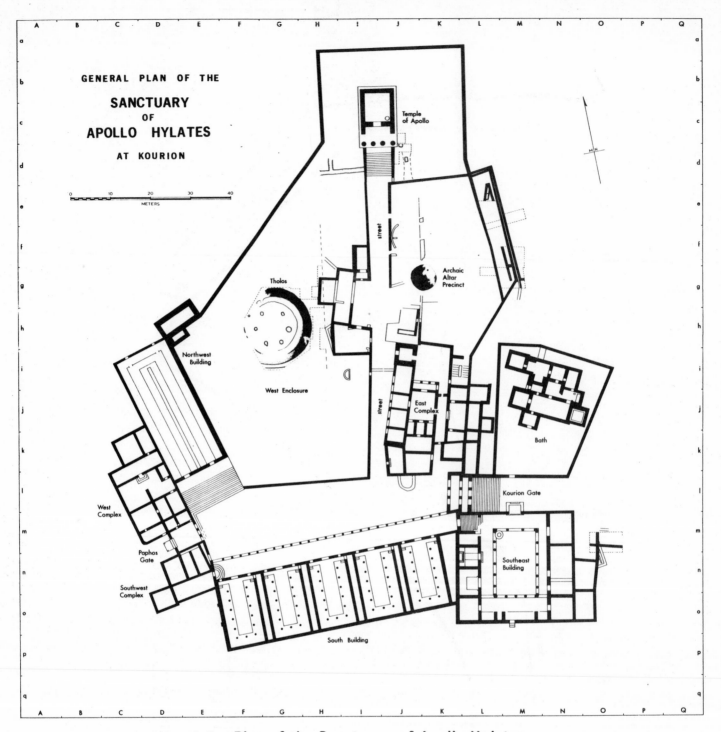

6-2. Plan of the Sanctuary of Apollo Hylates.

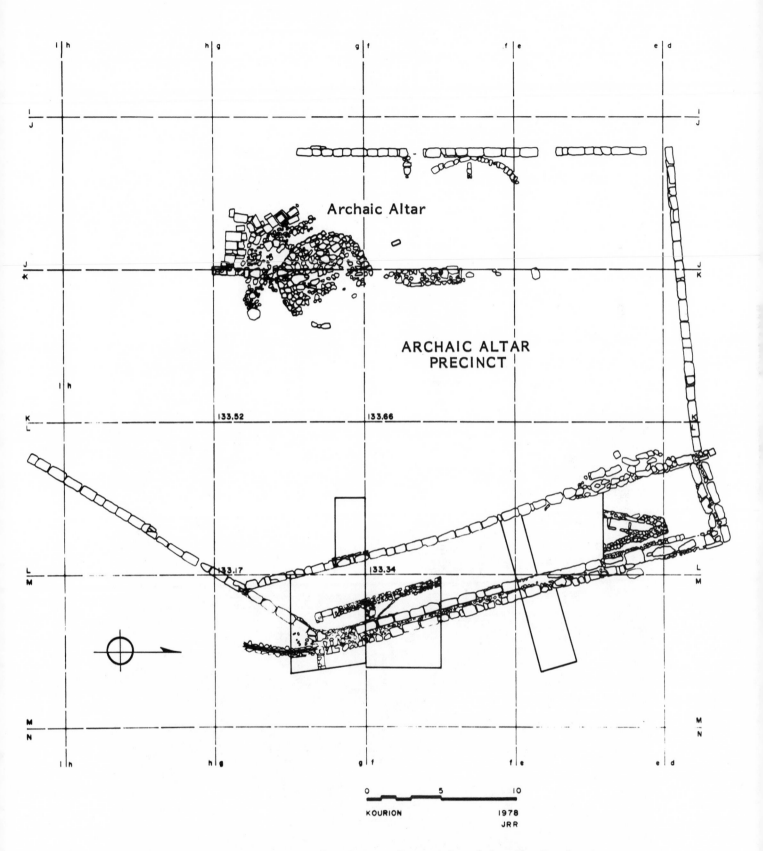

6-3. Plan of the Archaic Precinct. Drawn by John Rutherford.

6-4. Robert Scranton standing on the circular rubble altar in the
Archaic Precinct with "Fence Post" in the foreground at left.
Photo by John Huffstot.

6-5. Gold Figurine of a bull, actual size. Photo by John Huffstot.

6-6. Silver figurine of a bull, actual size. Photo by John Huffstot.

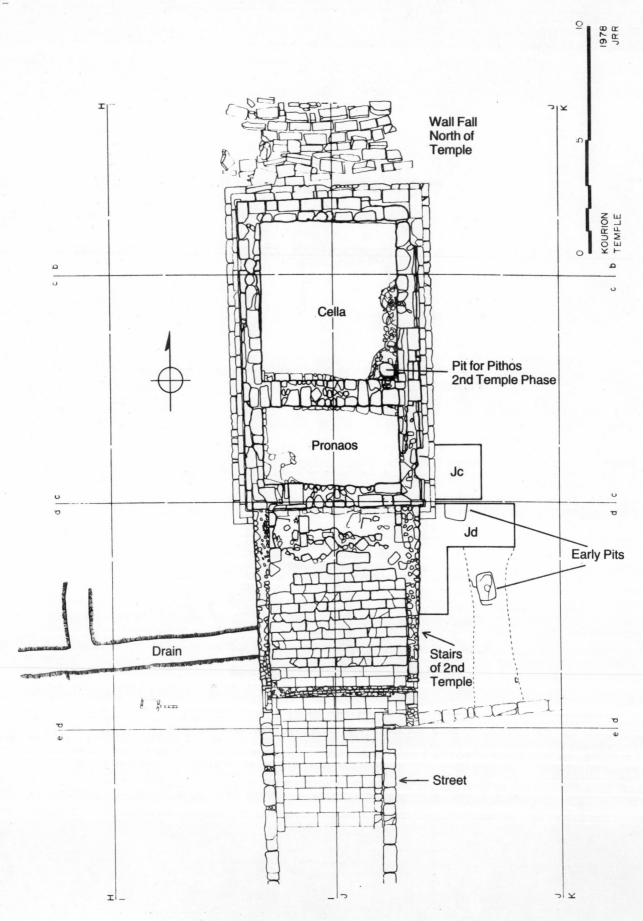

Wall Fall
North of
Temple

Cella

Pit for Pithos
2nd Temple Phase

Pronaos

Jc

Jd

Early Pits

Drain

Stairs
of 2nd
Temple

Street

KOURION TEMPLE

1978
JRR

6-7. Plan of the Temple of Apollo. Drawn by John Rutherford.

6-8. Blocks from the north wall of the Temple of Apollo lying as they fell during an earthquake. Photo by John Rutherford and John Huffstot.

0 1 2 3 4 5
METERS

Proposed Partial Reconstruction of the Façade (South Elevation) of the
Temple of Apollo Hylates at Kourion

6-9.

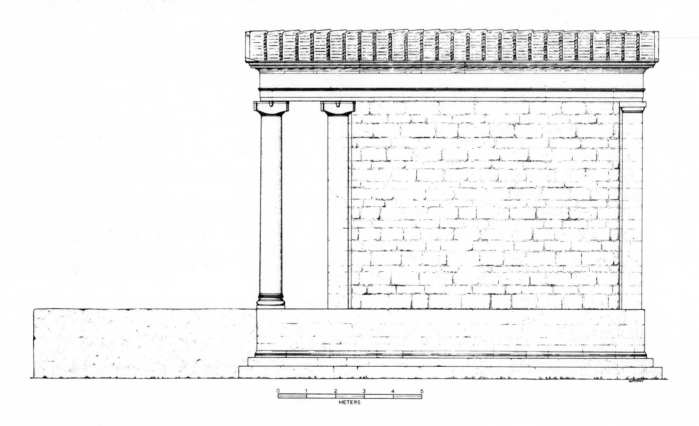

Proposed Partial Reconstruction of the East Elevation of the
Temple of Apollo Hylates at Kourion

6-10.

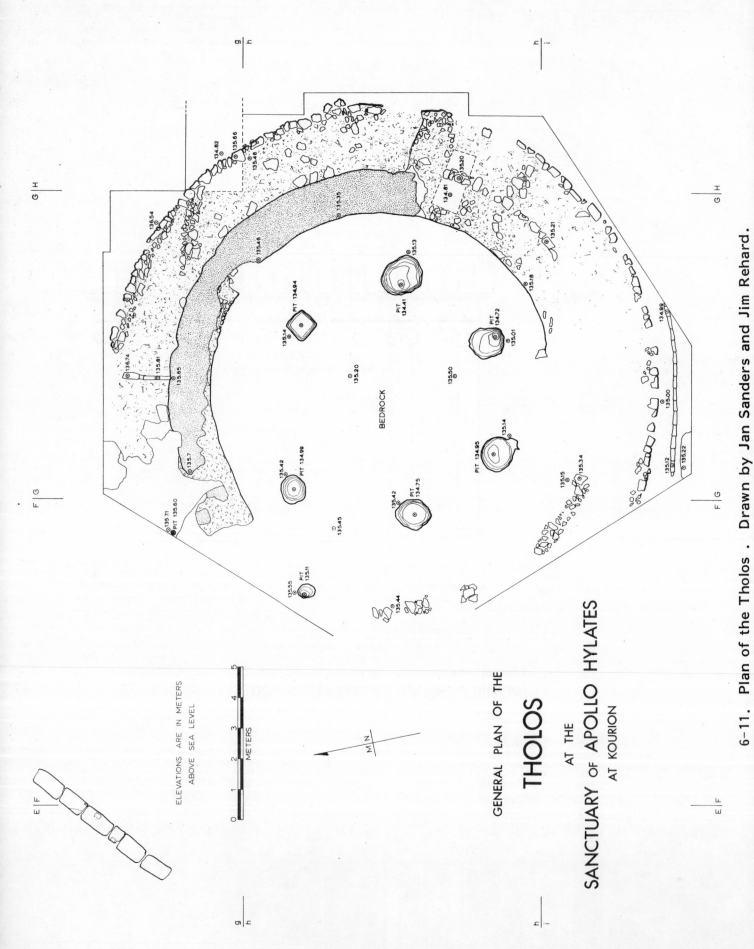

GENERAL PLAN OF THE

THOLOS

AT THE

SANCTUARY of APOLLO HYLATES

AT KOURION

6-11. Plan of the Tholos . Drawn by Jan Sanders and Jim Rehard.

6-12. View of the Tholos from north and above. Photo by David McAllister.

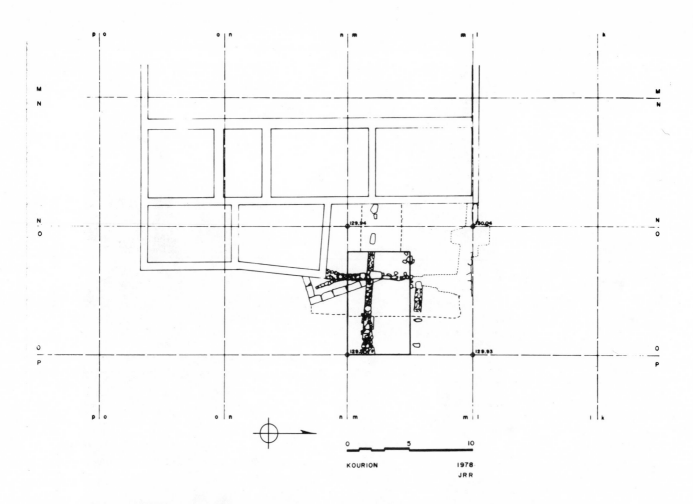

6-13. **Plan of the squatter occupation in square Om east of the Southeast Building. Drawn by John Rutherford.**

6-14. **Earthquake debris mounded up east of the Southeast Building in square Om, from the northeast.**

CHAPTER 7.

EARTHQUAKE: THE LAST DAYS OF KOURION

David Soren

The Sanctuary of Apollo Hylates at Kourion came to a dramatic and violent end by earthquake, and, from all appearances, this occurred at one moment in time:

> Most of the buildings were literally laid out
> flat where they remained essentially until the
> time of the excavations (Scranton 1967:74)

After three years of investigating this quake and its debris in and around the sanctuary, some important new conclusions have been reached and are documented here:

1. The widely believed idea that Kourion city and the
    Apollo Sanctuary were destroyed by earthquake between
    325-350 A.D. is untrue.

2. The attempt to link the final Kourion quake with quakes
    at Soli or Salamis cannot be substantiated.

3. The final earthquake occurred no earlier than 364 A.D.
    and most likely very close to 370 A.D.

4. The final earthquake was part of a series of shocks which
    occurred over several years and may have rendered the
    area unsafe for habitation.

5. The major damage resulted from a massive shear wave which
    ended the life of the sanctuary.

6. This quake was so disastrous that it was known even
    to non-Cypriotes.

7. The epicenter of the quake may be plotted roughly, allowing for a good margin of error and showing great caution.

8. The intensity of the quake may be estimated.

9. The supposed epicenter agrees well with contemporary geological fault areas.

10. An earlier quake may have occurred in the period of 330 to 340 A.D. and may have done limited damage to the sanctuary.

This archaeological detective story begins with an analysis of earthquake affected strata in the sanctuary. The most obvious area is the Temple of Apollo itself where fallen blocks of walls have been found extensively to the north (Figure 6-8) and east of the building, while little evidence of debris west of the temple was noted either in the recent excavations or by the previous excavator, George McFadden.

This analysis is significant because, if one can determine the direction of the orderly fall of debris from a building, it is possible to determine approximately the direction of the earthquake's epicenter. Thus, if quake debris falls to the north and east, the epicenter should normally be somewhere to the southwest. This would indeed correspond very well with the modern earthquake epicenters off the coast of Cyprus.

The area east of the temple was full of scattered and tumbled blocks with only a few preserved as they apparently fell. The lone preserved capital from the temple (Scranton 1967:22) was also found to the east, along with a large number of roof tiles (McFadden 1935-53:311). But the blocks of the north area proved to have fallen in precise rows and were still little disturbed (Figure 6-8).

According to Dr. Reuben Bullard, Professor of Geology at Cincinnati Bible College, an intense quake occurred and was followed soon after by a seismic pulse, the very destructive second or shear wave which had the power to throw down whole walls containing large ashlar blocks. To photograph this northern area it was possible to use a bipod designed by Julian Whittlesy (and used under the super-vision of project architect John Rutherford) to show how the upper part of the north wall of the temple collapsed.

According to Dr. J.P. Neophytou, geophysicist for the Cyprus Geological Service in Nicosia, an earthquake which could strike with such a force would have measured "possibly a nine" on the modified Mercalli Scale. He said that the quake would have had enough power, if it had struck in Washington, D.C., to knock over the Capitol building. Obviously it was a major seismic event which would have stood out signif-icantly in this historical period.

Many other areas around the site showed evidence of quake damage. In the Southeast Building or palaestra (Figure 6-2), McFadden found collapsed walls, some of which were laid out so perfectly that he could reerect them. He also found much associated statuary, coins, roof tiles, and assorted debris.

In 1978 and 1979, a structure appended to the palaestra at the east was excavated (Figure 6-13). At first, it appeared to be an annex, but it is now clear that it was a post-quake squatter construction made up largely of quake debris and dating not earlier than the end of the 5th century after Christ at a time when the sanctuary had long been in disuse. All kinds of debris appeared in the fill which had been brought in from the immediate vicinity to make a statumen for a now missing floor. A large number of roof tiles, shaped boulders, and mortar was excavated, and even a large block of caliche (the solution weathering of carbonate bedrock) of the same size and configuration as that of a reconstructed windowsill in the northwest area of the palaestra was found.

Beneath this late level, which is useful only for giving some idea of the extent of destruction and for showing that it was never possible to rebuild the sanctuary, was a white floor of pure, fine, white caliche which was probably installed shortly after the great quake. It may have marked part of a road laid at the extreme south-east end of the collapsed sanctuary or it may be part of some squatter construction of the later 4th century. A stable in the northwest room of the palaestra is further proof of the primitive, but extensive, re-use of the area in post quake times, but, since the stable was dug out by McFadden and the evidence never published, the date is still unknown.

The South Building, (Figure 6-2) as excavated by McFadden, also showed evidence of quake collapse with its colonnaded front hurled to the northeast. Another area at grid Hg3 was dug out by McFadden, who left in section a series of ashlar blocks which Dr. Bullard suggests came from eastward quake fall from the west wall of the exedra of the Central Court.

The most significant area of quake fall proved to be in one of the less important structures of the site: the West Complex (Figure 6-2). McFadden used this area to substantiate his conclusion that the disastrous quake occurred in the period 325-350 A.D.:

> Much debris was removed before finding the
> floor levels in the propylon and West Building.
> This consisted mainly of tiles and rough undressed
> stones   (McFadden 1940:25).

McFadden discovered a good deal of debris in the porch of the propylon and in the court east of it. Here and in the West Building proper there was only a beaten earth floor under which he notes "the absence of debris" (McFadden 1940:25).

In his Rooms 3 to 7 he found under the quake debris "a layer of fallen clay mixed with chavara varying in depth from ten to twenty-two centimeters which is explained as having fallen from the roof or from an upper floor." He added:

> In Room 3 it occurs directly over a paved floor.
> As is the practice today in Cypriote rural archi-
> tecture, the clay would have been laid over reed
> matting supported on beams   (McFadden 1940:27).

In short, McFadden found intact a sealed area of collapse on top of earthen (and in a few cases paved) floors. Thus, he realized that the objects trapped here should date the great quake, and the fact that no debris was found in or under the floor lent support to this idea.

He cited a large number of coins found in Room 2 and one under the debris of Room 4:

> The many coins...appear to belong to the early
> fourth century; these are now in the course of
> being studied. Three lamps (Broneer Type 28)
> found on the late floor level just over the rock
> in Room 5, and under the clay; and fragments of
> the same type under the debris in other rooms,
> confirm the evidence of the coins (McFadden
> 1940:28).

Having made his estimate of the date of the quake, he suggested that the same quake was felt in such places as Soli on the north coast which supposedly fell in the period 325-350, "so the earthquake may well have occurred in the second quarter of the century" (McFadden 1940:28).

This date, in the years since McFadden's report of 1940, has been accepted by scholars as accurate. Professor Scranton wrote in 1967:

> It was not until the second quarter of the fourth
> century that the end came and its effects were com-
> plete....The date is assured by large numbers of
> coins found in the debris though precision is elu-
> sive because there was some activity on the site
> by squatters in the years shortly following
> (Scranton 1967: 74-75).

In the guidebook, *Romantic Cyprus,* Keshishian (1977:79) states simply that "... sanctuary buildings were destroyed by earthquake in 350 A.D." A bit more cautious is the official Kourion guide, published by the Cypriote Department of Antiquities, which tells of destruction "by earthquakes probably in the fourth century A.D." (Curium 1961:10).

Serious objections must be raised (after 42 years) to McFadden's conclusions. First, he promised a detailed study of the coins but this was not carried out in context. When Dorothy Cox published the coins of Kourion, she observed most sur-prisingly:

> Although occupied from the eighth century B.C.
> to about the end of the fourth century A.D.
> there was little stratification of use in dating
> coins. In fact nowhere at Kourion was there any
> important stratigraphy, nothing to show the
> growth or decline of the city (Cox 1959:ix).

Without archaeological contexts in her book, it is impossible to know which coins came from the debris layers.

McFadden also cited the presence under the fallen clay of coins dating to the reign of Constantius II (346-361):

> In the propylon court on the rock at the foot
> of the threshold was found a coin of Constantius II
> (McFadden 1940:28).

At this point he refers to Plate VII in his text, but there the coin which he has just identified is labeled "Constantine II," and the coin itself is not visible in the plate.

This may be a typographic error, but certainly it is a critical one since it throws the entire article into confusion. He also cites another quake area at the Kourion city site where an excavation by Professor Daniel in 1934 revealed another coin of Constantius II, along with two female skeletons and Broneer Type 28 lamps.

Thus the McFadden article exhibits a basic flaw in logic. How could a quake assigned to 325-350 A.D. have sealed debris which, at its very earliest, dates to 346 A.D. At this point, with the date of the final quake left uncertain, it became necessary to find the actual coins cited in the McFadden field diary. After a two-week search of the Episkopi Museum and storerooms the coins were located by Christofis Polycarpou, museum supervisor, Kourion Museum. They were cleaned by Terry Weisser, Chief of Conservation, of The Walters Art Gallery, with striking results.

No fewer than 29 coins were recovered from the West Complex and are published in detail at the end of this article. The legible coins dated principally from the 350s and 360s A.D. The layer thus cannot be dated before 364 A.D. and is probably datable to about 370 A.D.

Twenty-two coins were definitely found in sealed quake areas. Of those which could be identified, six were of emperor Constantius II, three appeared to be coins of that emperor, two were either Valens or Valentinian I, one appeared to be Valens, three appeared to be Valentinian I, one was definitely Valentinian I, and one was of Constantius Gallus. It is also important to note that McFadden found coins in fill under the floor on which the quake debris was found, and these coins differed completely in date from those found above, belonging to the 320s and 330s, suggesting that about 335 A.D., or a bit later, the last floor before the quake was installed in the West Complex. The coins include an Urbs Roma issue, as well as two coins of Constantius II as Caesar, one of Constantinus II, and an earlier sestertius of Antoninus Pius.

This means that, at the time McFadden posited his final quake, the West Complex was given a late floor and was, in fact, still standing with no real evidence of great quake damage or massive collapse in the layers. This does not rule out the possibility that a quake of ca. 335 or a bit later could have been felt at Kourion and even done some damage. In fact, in Room 2, at the bottom of the fifth stratum, a layer of fill belonging to the packing for the last floor in the West House, a floor was found showing "traces of fire in the center" (McFadden 1935-53:538).

It would be presumptuous to attempt to overturn McFadden's conclusions about the final destruction of the sanctuary on the basis of only one spot which he excavated. But he himself reported finding at the city site of Kourion evidence of "a coin of Constantius II..." in a destroyed house. It was "... found on the floor, near the skeleton remains of two women caught in the earthquake that brought down the house" (McFadden 1940:28).

However, it would be even more conclusive to find one other area at Kourion where a date around 370 A.D. might be attested. In fact, the answer came from an important article on the theater of the city of Kourion by Richard Stillwell in 1961. Stillwell was convinced of the traditional arguments for the date of the final quake (i.e., 325-350 A.D.). Yet his evidence for the destruction of the theater confirmed the conclusions that the event had occurred in approximately 370 A.D.:

> Two violent earthquakes in the early thirties
> and forties of the fourth century were recorded
> for Salamis. These may well mark the end of the
> Curium theater. In any case, the latest coins

> found in the rooms behind the center of the
> stage building, underneath piles of fallen
> blocks, are of Valentinian and Valens
> (Stillwell 1961:78).

Stillwell's discovery that the theater was, in fact, standing until the time of Valentinian and Valens agrees with the findings, and his argument that quakes at Salamis would have affected Kourion may still be true, but to a much lesser degree than had been supposed.

Stillwell also discussed the quake fall in the area of shops just south of the stage building:

> That they continued to serve for a con-
> siderable time, probably until the destruction
> of the theater, is attested by coins found in
> their ruins. The latest, in Room S. 1, occurring
> a little above floor level, is of Valentinian I
> (Valens), about A.D. 372. A similar coin
> was found on the floor of Room T4, so that
> from the evidence the theater and the buildings
> adjacent to it were destroyed in the last half
> of the fourth century (Stillwell 1961:62-63).

He was not alone in pointing out differences in date from McFadden's conclusions.

Terence Mitford offered in his text, first of all, the standard McFadden interpretation:

> Accordingly, like Paphos, Kourion was never
> fully restored after devastation by the earth-
> quakes of the early fourth century--her theater
> abandoned, her Sanctuary of Apollo at Hyle
> not converted but left desolate (Mitford 1971:351).

But he clearly had second thoughts, expressed in a footnote, when he said that his conclusion was reached "on the assumption, perhaps somewhat perilous, that Kourion suffered devastation from these earthquakes comparable to that of Paphos."

While it is true that much of Cyprus was struck by quakes in the first half of the 4th century, the Kourion area is never cited in the ancient texts. Salamis on the east coast was severely hit in 332-333 A.D. and again in 342; Soli may have been struck on the north coast in 324 A.D., while Paphos was said to be destroyed about 342 A.D.[1] But these were separate events, and it is not at all necessary that quakes affecting these areas so completely need have done more than superficial, or perhaps a bit more than superficial, damage at Kourion. Dr. J.P. Neophytou, Geophysicist with the Cyprus Geological Survey, confirms that the site of Kourion, 30 miles from Paphos and 80 from Salamis, could have escaped more lightly than McFadden had believed possible, and the evidence is now clear that major structures at Kourion did not fall in these earlier quakes.

From the degree of damage done by the quake and the tendency of the debris at the Apollo Sanctuary to fall to the north and east, Dr. Reuben Bullard evaluated the quake as a nine or ten in intensity when estimated on the Mercalli Scale, a preseismograph evaluating technique still used on Cyprus. On the Modified Mercalli Intensity Scale, an eight indicates that chimneys, factory stacks, columns, monuments, and walls would fall; heavy furniture would be overturned; and sand and mud ejected in small amounts. A nine means that buildings would be shifted off their foundations, underground pipes broken, and the ground cracked conspicuously, while a ten includes bad cracking of the ground and landslides.

The West House, Temple of Apollo, palaestra, and South Building at the Sanctuary of Apollo, and the theater and its shops at the city site a mile away were demolished. It is now possible to attribute the demise of the so-called gymnasium of Kourion, currently being excavated by Demos Christou, to this period as well. Unpublished finds show that predebris floor repairs were carried out in that building in the first half of the 4th century after Christ, perhaps another indication of repairs after some minor quake damage. In the north area of Kourion the archaeologist Mr. Loulloupis, staff member of the Cyprus Museum, Nicosia, and Director of Cypriote excavations at Amathus, kindly pointed out most spectacular quake dislodgements of ground level of up to 1 m., actual cracks in the earth which appreciably displaced buildings and utterly destroyed them. This latter material is still unpublished.

Dr. Neophytou assesses the quake as "probably a nine, but possibly higher."[2] Geologist Frank Koucky, consulted by the author in 1978, first suggested that the direction of fall of the quake debris could be significant. Fall from the shear wave to the north and east would suggest an epicenter to the southwest. Dr. Bullard cautioned against pinpointing the epicenter without gathering more data from a number of different quake affected sites with datable strata.

Dr. Neophytou agreed that the epicenter was probably to the southwest and, after studying the modern offshore fault lines, suggested that the epicenter of the ancient quake was generally in the area of latitude 34 degrees 30 minutes and longitude 32 degrees 30 minutes. Roughly translated, this would be some 35 km. southwest of the Temple of Apollo or 20 km. south of Petra tou Romiou (Aphrodite's Rock) (Figure 7-1). Dr. Bullard suggests that the epicenter may have been slightly further away, but did not offer coordinates.

Dr. Neophytou has been compiling a corpus of ancient Cypriote quakes and has allowed the author to draw on his work for the purposes of this article. He has amended his work to include the new evidence, namely that an enormously destructive quake ended the life of Kourion about 370 A.D. and that it may have been accompanied by other quakes which could have continued at intervals over a number of years. McFadden observed:

> That none returned to retrieve or bury the dead
> testifies to the magnitude and extent of the
> earthquake (McFadden 1940:28).

Lamps found in the possession of the trapped, abandoned skeletons suggest that the individuals were trying to escape, quite likely at night. It may be that the area was unsafe for a considerable period of time.

With these ideas in mind, it is instructive to examine some of the literary evidence for earthquakes at the time under consideration. Ambraseys (1960:3) attempted to summarize the seismic history of Cyprus, including "all those shocks which seem to have an undoubted origin in and about the island and for which sufficient, although not always conclusive information was found."

Ambraseys' entry for the year 370 A.D. is so startling in light of the present findings that it bears reproducing here:

370:   Soon after (342 A.D.), one or more earthquakes
shook Cyprus again.   The dates of these events are
difficult to ascertain.   Ammianus gives 378 and
from Fabricius and Siever we gather that this should
have happened before 380 and most probably about
367.   It is very likely that what we have here is a
series of earthquakes which shook Cyprus between 365
and 378.   It seems probable that the first shock was
from the earthquake   of 21st July 365 which caused
considerable damage in Greece, Crete, Asia Minor and
Egypt.   Another shock occurred probably in 367 followed by a strong earthquake in 375 A.D.   This shock
was mostly felt in Crete and in the neighboring
islands...It is, however, very probable that these
shocks caused considerable damage in Cyprus, and
also that they continued for some time, perhaps between 364 and 375.   One or more of these earthquakes
marked the end of the theater at Curium.   The latest
coins found at Curium were in the room behind the
stage building, underneath piles of fallen blocks and
are of Valentinian and Valens.   The accumulative
effects of these earthquakes in Cyprus seem to be
considerable, particularly in Paphos and in the area
of Akrotiri   (ibid.:6).

The evidence uncovered in 1979 demonstrates that two sites, the city of Kourion
and the Sanctuary of Apollo, were destroyed by a series of earthquakes ca. 370
A.D. and left uninhabitable for some time.   The archaeological, literary, and seismo-
logical arguments agree well.   These quakes were so destructive that word of the
disaster spread around the Mediterranean as an example of a people struck by in-
credible suffering.

After working in the debris for so long, one finds it difficult not to be moved
by the second oration (chapter 52) of Libanius, who wrote in approximately
380 A.D. while the memory of disaster was still fresh:

ἀλλ' ἐμοὶ μὲν τοὺς συναχθομένους εἰ καὶ πλεῖστον ἀπέχοιεν τῶν περὶ
λόγους φιλῶ, τοὺς δ' ἐν ἑτέροις ζῶντας εἰ μὴ τῶν αὐτῶν ἀξιοίην οὐκ
ἀδικήσω;   οὐκ ἐσμὲν Κύπριοι οὐδέ, σὺν Ἀδραστείᾳ δὲ εἰρήσεται, τῷ σεισμῷ
κατενεχθεῖσαν ἐπείδομεν τὴν πόλιν, ἀλλ' ὅμως οἰμωγαὶ καὶ ὀδυρμοί, καὶ
ὢ πόλεις, ποῦ ποτε ἄρ' ἐστε;   πολλῶν ἦν ἀκούειν λεγόντων, καὶ οὐδεὶς
ἐπέπληξεν εἰ τοσαύτῃ τῆς νήσου διειργόμενοι τῇ θαλάσσῃ μετέχειν τῆς
συμφορᾶς ἐνομίζομεν.

Those who sympathize with me in my grief, however far removed they may be from the world of
learning, receive my affection.   Will I not be
doing injustice to people in other walks of life, if
I refuse to accord them the same.   We are not
Cypriotes, nor yet, and may heaven forbid, have
we beheld our city laid low by earthquake.   But
still there you could hear many people moaning,
lamenting: 'Alas, poor cities!   Where on earth
are you now?'   And no one has reproved us for
thinking that we shared in the disaster, though
separated by such a stretch of sea.

APPENDIX

Coins from the Earthquake Fall of the West House

On April 8, 1936, and again between May 10 and 13, 1939, George McFadden conducted excavations in the West House which brought to light some 29 bronze coins, 22 of which were in strata sealed by earthquake collapse. Some of these coins were referred to in his 1940 publication, but many were never cleaned and the precise relationship to their context never fully discussed. After 40 years, these coins and their strata give strong evidence of an earthquake ca. 370 A.D. and also suggest that a new floor was installed in at least one of the rooms before the quake, sometime in or shortly after 335 A.D.

Each room is discussed here with regard to the strata found by McFadden, and each coin is identified as completely as possible.

ROOM 1

Room 1 of the West House produced two coins. Stratum one in McFadden's trench consisted of loose surface soil and debris, so that it could not be identified as a true sealed earthquake layer. Stratum two, however, was a definite quake layer containing many stones, late pots, and a Doric capital resting on the floor (stratum three) of the room.

Stratum One - (McFadden 1935-53:532), found May 12, 1939

1. C253 - (C547) Aes 3 or 4, diameter ca. 17 mm.
346-361 A.D.

Obverse - May be diademed bust of Constantius II.

Reverse - FEL TEMP REPARATIO. Soldier spearing.
Exergue: SMANT, mint of Antioch.

Stratum Two - (McFadden 1935-53:495), found April 8, 1936

2. C108 - (C564) Aes 4, diameter 14 mm.
Found on the floor under stratum two.

Constantius II, 346-361 A.D.

Obverse - DN CONSTANTIUS PF AUG. Diademed bust.

Reverse - FEL TEMP REPARATIO (Hill, Carson and
Kent 1965: Type III). Soldier spearing
fallen horseman.

ROOM 2

Room 2 contained the vast majority of the earthquake coins and is discussed primarily on pages 499 and 522 of McFadden's diary (McFadden 1935-53). Stratum one was surface soil, and stratum two was fallen debris with a large number of stones and roof tiles. Stratum three had a "floor on the bottom and few stones." It was similar to stratum three of Room 1, in and on which were found complete pots. Thus, Room 2, stratum three was a sealed quake layer which had many coins: "On and over floor of Room 2 north center were found a mass of coins." This group was found "all near or on floor according to the workman who found them."

Stratum four was a layer of fill under the floor on which the quake debris was sealed, and finds from this stratum date the construction of the last floor in Room 2 before the great quake occurred. It contained no debris and consisted of reddish brown loose earth. This room was excavated on May 10 to 13 of 1939.

Finally, beneath stratum four was a harder fill of reddish brown earth which might have been more of the fourth stratum more tightly compacted.

Stratum Three - (McFadden 1935-53:499, 522), found May 10, 1939

3. C244 - (C540) Aes 4, diameter 13 mm.
   Found on the bottom of the third stratum; marked illegible by McFadden.

   Obverse - Bust, possibly of Constantius II.

   Reverse - Male figure? Rest illegible, may be a
   FEL TEMP type.

4. C242 - (C539) Aes 3, diameter 17 mm. (Figure 7-2)
   Found stuck together with number 5; marked illegible by McFadden. This coin and numbers 5, 8 through 17, and 21 were found just over or on the floor (stratum four) near the north wall halfway between the east and west walls.

   Obverse - ...AL...Appears to be Valens or
   possibly Valentinian I portrait bust.

   Reverse - Victory moving left holding wreath
   and apparently a palm.

5. C243 - (C539) Aes 3, diameter 17 mm.
   Similar to preceding coin.

   Obverse - Portrait head appears similar to the
   preceding entry.

   Reverse - Same as preceding entry. Legend SECURITAS
   identifies this as a Securitas Rei Publicae
   issue, common under the emperors cited
   in the preceding entry, beginning 364
   or 365 A.D.

6. C228 – (C537) Aes 3, diameter 17 mm.
    Found in the bottom of the stratum with numbers 7 and 20;
    marked illegible by McFadden.

    Obverse – Pearl diademed bust close to Valentinian I,
        but legend not decipherable.

    Reverse – Like previous entry, but illegible
        legend.

7. C229 – (C537) Aes 3 or 4, diameter 17 mm.
    Marked illegible by McFadden.
    Constantius II, 355–361 A.D.

    Obverse – Diademed bust with legend ...TIUS PF AUG.

    Reverse – Standing figure with spear and globe.
        SPES REIPUBLICAE. Exergue: CONSPA
        (Constantinple Pecunia).

8. C239 – (C538) Aes 3 or 4, diameter 17 mm.
    Found with numbers 18 and 19.
    May be Constantius II, 346–361 A.D.

    Obverse – Bust similar to Constantius II, CONSTAN...

    Reverse – Poorly preserved, possibly a FEL TEMP
        REPARATIO type with soldier spearing
        falling horseman.

9. C241 – (C538) Aes 3, diameter 18 mm.
    Constantius II, 355–361 A.D.
    (Hill, et al. 1965: no. 2049)

    Obverse – DN CONSTAN... Diademed bust.

    Reverse – FEL TEMP REPARATIO. Soldier spearing fallen
        horseman. Exergue: ...NSA for Constantinople M
        in field.

10. C238 – (C538) Aes 4, diameter 13 mm.
    Constantius II, 351–361 A.D.

    Obverse – ...TIUS PFA... Bust of Constantius II.

    Reverse – Soldier spearing fallen horseman.
        Exergue: CON... for Constantinople.

11. C236 – (C538) Illegible, diameter 11 mm.

12. C237 – (C538) Illegible, diameter 12 mm.

13.   C235 - (C538) Virtually illegible, diameter 13 mm.

Obverse - Bust poorly preserved.

Reverse - Virtually illegible, but may be a Victory
moving left resembling number 15 here.

14.   C240 - (C538) Aes 2 Centenionalis, diameter 20 mm.
Constantius Gallus, 351-354 A,D,

Obverse - ...CONSTANTIUS NOB CAES. Bare headed bust.

Reverse - FEL TEMP REPARATIO (hill et a. 1965: Type III).
Soldier spearing fallen horseman.

15.   C249 - (C543) Aes 3 or 4, diameter 15 mm.
Valentinian I?, 364-375 A.D.

Obverse - Close to number 6, a virtually identical
diademed bust.

Reverse - Victory moving left with palm and wreath.
Legend illegible.

16.   C247 - (C542) Aes 3 or 4, diameter 17 mm.
Found stuck to the following entry.
Constantius II, 346-361 A.D.

Obverse - DN CONS... Diademed bust.

Reverse - FEL TEMP REPARATIO. Soldier spearing
fallen horseman.

17.   C248 - (C542) Aes 3, diameter 17 mm. (Figure 7-3).
Valentinian I, 364-375 A.D.

Obverse - DN VALENTINIANUS PF AUG. Diademed bust.

Reverse - Valentinian advancing right and dragging
captive, probably a Gloria Romanorum type
beginning 364 or 365 A.D.

18.   C245 - (C541) Aes 3 or 4, diameter 15 mm.
Found stuck to the following entry. Later 4th century.

Obverse - Illegible.

Reverse - Victory advancing left with palm branch and
wreath.

19.   C246 - (C541) Aes 3, diameter 17 mm.
Valens?, 364-378 A.D.

Obverse - ...PF AUG. Diademed bust. Legend
arrangement strongly suggests Valens.

Reverse – Poorly preserved, but similar to preceding entry.

20.   C227 – (C536) Aes 3, diameter 16 mm. Valentinian I ?, 364 A.D. or after.

Obverse – Diademed bust poorly preserved, but very similar to number 6.

Reverse – Similar to number 17. Emperor moves right with labarum and drags captive.

21.   C249A – (C543) Illegible

Stratum Four – May 12-13, 1939

22.   C252 – (C546) Aes 3, diameter 18 mm. On fifth stratum near north wall. 335-337 A.D.

Obverse – URBS ROMA. Bust of Roma.

Reverse – Suckling she-wolf and twins with two stars. Exergue: SMANΘ, mint of Antioch (Sutherland and Carson 1966:697, no. 113; Cox 1959:49, no. 394).

23.   C251 – (C545) Aes 3, diameter 18 mm. Found on the floor of stratum five a few centimeters from the following entry. Constantius II as Caesar, 324-330 A.D.

Obverse – ...CONSTANTIUS NOB C. Bust of Caesar.

Reverse – PROVIDENTIAE CAESS. Camp gate with two turrets and arched entry with star above. Exergue: SMHГ, mint of Heraclea (Sutherland and Carson 1966:551, no. 78; Hill et al. 1965:22; Cox 1959:53).

24.   C250 – (C544) Aes 3 or 4, diameter 17 mm. Constantius II as Caesar, 330-335 A.D.

Obverse – ...S NOB C. Bust of Caesar.

Reverse – GLORIA EXERCITUS. Two soldiers flank two military standards. Exergue: SMKA, mint of Cyzicus (Sutherland and Carson 1966:655, no. 85; Hill et al. 1965:28, no. 1229).

Stratum Five

25.   C254 – (C548) Aes 3 or 4, diameter 17 mm. Found on sixth stratum. Constantinus II, 330-335 A.D.

Obverse – CONSTANTINUS IUN NOB C. Bust of Caesar

Reverse – As preceding entry but with exergue SMANA...,
   mint of Antioch (Hill et al. 1965:30)

26.   C257 – (C551) Sestertius, diameter 28 mm.
Found on sixth stratum in southeast corner of room.
Antoninus Pius, 150–151 A.D.

   Obverse – IMP CAES T AEL HADR ANTONINUS AUG PIUS PP.
      Bust of emperor.

   Reverse – TR POT X... Seated Annona with modius at
      feet, cornucopia on chair.
      Exergue: ANNONA AUG.

ROOM 3

Room 3 was excavated on May 10, 1939 (McFadden 1935–53:527). The first stratum contained loose surface soil, as well as fallen debris, including stones and tiles. Stratum two was a paved floor below the debris layer.

Stratum One – may not be sealed

27.   C225 – (C534) Follis, diameter 26 mm.
Found about 60 cm. below modern ground level.
Maximianus, 299–305 A.D.

   Obverse – IMP MAXIMIANUS PF AUG. Laureate bust
      jugate with bust of Hercules.

   Reverse – GENIO POPULI ROMANI. Genius stands left
      with patera. Exergue: SIS, mint of Siscia.
      1B in field (Sutherland and Carson 1966:467,
      no. 108b).

Stratum Two – (McFadden 1935–53:538).

28.   C259 – (C554) Aes 2, diameter 17 mm.
Found in the "2nd stratum on about three centimeters of earth on pieces of tile in crack in threshold lying flat and under fallen roof" (McFadden 1935–53:550). This associates the coin with the quake debris. Constantius II, 351–354 A.D.

   Obverse – DN CONSTAN...Well preserved diademed bust.

   Reverse – FEL TEMP REPARATIO. Soldier spearing fallen horse-
      man. Exergue: ANA, mint of Antioch
      (Hill et al. 1965:100, no. 2625).

ROOM 6

Room 6 was already partly dug in 1938 (McFadden 1935-53:521). The first stratum was a mix of the previously dug surface soil and fallen debris, while the second
was quake debris described as "a hard white fill, probably decomposing building
mortar" containing "late sherds."

Stratum Two

29. C258 - (C552) Aes 3 or 4, diameter 15 mm.
Found on the bottom of the second stratum on the floor.
Constantius II?, 346-361 A.D.

Obverse - Appears to be a bust of Constantius II.

Reverse - Illegible.

TALLY

If the coins are divided into prequake and quake debris coins, they appear as
follows:

A. Prequake Coins in Fill for Late Floor - 335 A.D. or
shortly after

1. Urbs Roma, 335-337 A.D. (no. 22)

2. Constantius II as Caesar, 324-330 A.D. (no. 23)

3. Constantius II as Caesar, 330-335 A.D. (no. 24)

4. Constantinus II, 330-335 A.D. (no. 25)

5. Antoninus Pius, 150-151 A.D. (no. 26)

B. Earthquake Coins - sealed securely in quake fall ca.
370 A.D.

1. Constantius II ?, 346-361 A.D. (nos. 3, 8, 29)

2. Constantius II, 346-361 A.D. (nos. 2, 16)

3. Constantius II, 351-354 A.D. (no. 28)

4. Constantius II, 351-361 A.D. (no. 10)

5. Constantius II, 355-361 A.D. (nos. 7, 9)

6. Constantius Gallus, 351-354 A.D. (no. 14)

7. Valens or Valentinian I, 364-378 A.D. (nos. 4, 5)

8. Valentinian I?, 364-375 A.D. (nos. 6, 15, 20)

9. Valens?, 364-378 A.D. (no. 19)

10. Valentinian I, 364-375 A.D. (no. 17)

NOTES

1. A possible quake of 76-77 A.D. is discussed by McFadden (1952b:588). For accounts of the ancient earthquakes of Cyprus, see Ambraseys (1960: 1-26; 1965: 405-410), Christofidou (1969-1972:270).

2. Dr. Neophytou adds that, from a preliminary survey of the quake damage, he believes the epicenter was deeper than 70 km. below the surface, with a possible magnitude of eight or greater but that he would need more comparative material to confirm this. Earthquakes remain common on Cyprus, and Dr. Neophytou reported "a minor strong earthquake was felt all over Cyprus" on May 28, 1979, which caused people in some communities to "run to the streets" although no serious damage occurred.

ACKNOWLEDGMENTS

This article would not have been possible without the contributions of Vassos Karageorghis, Director of Antiquities; Reuben Bullard and Frank Koucky, geologists; J.P. Neophytou, geophysicist; Robert Scranton, architectural historian; and Eugene Lane, epigrapher, who, besides being general epigraphical consultant, also drew my attention to the passage in Libanius. I also wish to thank Demos Christou for permitting me to examine unpublished material from his excavations.

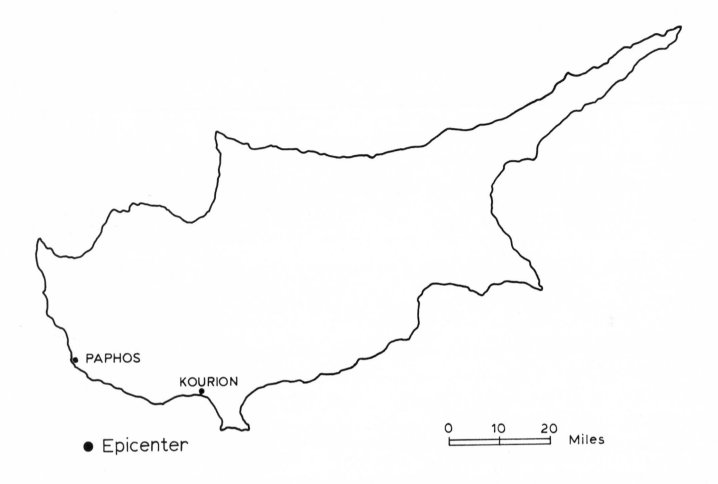

● Epicenter

0   10   20   Miles

7-1. Projected earthquake epicenter according to Dr. J.P. Neophytou.
Drawn by John Huffstot.

7-2. Bronze Coin of Valens or Valentinian, 364-378 A.D., no. 4. Scale 2:1.
Photo by John Huffstot.

7-3. Bronze coin of Valentinian I,
364-378 A.D., no. 17. Scale 2:1.
Photo by John Huffstot.

CHAPTER 8.

A BRONZE BELT FROM THE SANCTUARY OF APOLLO AT KOURION

Hillary Browne

Bronze belts are documented in the ancient world as early as the 3rd millennium B.C. (Moorey 1967:83). During the Iron Age (ca. 1050-500 B.C.), 9th century examples from Luristan are usually adorned with repoussé figures and animals and often have cable pattern borders (Dussaud 1934:192, fig.3, pl. 25; 1949: fig.10; Amiet 1968:225,257, figs. 4-6). Although never very common in the eastern Mediterranean area, bronze belts of Iron Age date are nevertheless found throughout the region (Boardman 1961/62:186-187). Those found in Ionia, Phrygia, and Greece are generally decorated with punched geometric designs (ibid.:180, 186, pl. 92, fig. 23; Curtius, Adler, and Hirschfeld 1966:48-49, pl. XIX, nos. 317-322; Benton 1953:340, 352, nos. E243, E243a, pl. 69; Stupka 1972:149-157). A belt from Crete with rounded ends and "figures embossed and traced upon it" is an exception which "copies Eastern models" (Boardman 1961/62:186). Ionian belts, the first of which was identified in 1955, come from reliable archaeological contexts and date to the 8th and 7th centuries (ibid.:187). There is good evidence, however, that this type of belt continued in use as late as the second quarter of the 6th century (Boardman 1967: 214).

A fragmentary bronze belt resembling examples from Luristan was excavated in 1978 on the site of the Sanctuary of Apollo Hylates at Kourion (Figures 8-1 and 8-2). Pieces of the belt were found at several different levels in an area of disturbed fill in the eastern sector of the Archaic Precinct near what is believed to be the temenos wall. Although the archaeological context contained a mixture of artifacts, Cypro-Archaic pottery and other objects of the 6th century B.C. predominated.

Executed in thin bronze and utilizing the repoussé technique with chased details, the piece depicts two lions attacking a griffin against a background of evenly spaced, stylized date palms. The upper and lower borders of the composition are framed with cable pattern. A few areas are difficult to interpret. The griffin's front legs, which should be visible below the wing, cannot be distinguished. Another uncertain area is the line of zigzags, flanked by solid borders, which swings across the shoulder and under the muzzle of the lion on the left. Although harnesses can be seen on lions from the Amarna period all the way down to the Siphnian Treasury frieze and beyond, this design is not correctly placed to represent one. Both lions and griffins are occasionally decorated with ribbons, but again, never in this manner. This feature must communicate with pieces of the belt which are no longer preserved and thus remains unexplained.

As products of diverse cultural influences, the antiquities of Cyprus have always afforded special difficulties in classification. The Kourion belt, although similar to the 9th century belts from Luristan in its use of repoussé animals and a cable pattern border, does not appear to have been made in Luristan. The use of the cable pattern is too widespread in date and provenance to help date and localize the Kourion belt (Potratz 1964:175-220). A stylistic analysis of its other decorative elements, however, suggests a date for this belt and indicates that it is probably of Cypriote manufacture.

The subject matter, a combat between a griffin and lions, is quite uncommon (Karageorghis 1973b:83), and the origin of the motif remains controversial. Barnett, in his publication of the Nimrud ivories (1975:36,74), postulates that it is a North Syrian creation on the evidence of second millennium B.C. glyptics. Porada, however, believes that scenes of lion and griffin battles are specifically Aegean in origin (Porada 1979:116, note 14). Whatever the source, it is likely that the Phoenicians disseminated this motif (Barnett 1975:76). A piece of engraved foil from Tyre with a lion and griffin combat and the ubiquitous cable pattern illustrates 14th century Phoenician work (Frankfort 1970:260, no. 301). Mycenaean ivory incised plaques from Delos are perhaps the finest surviving depictions of this theme (Gallet de Santerre and Tréheux 1947:pl. XXIX).

Closer in locale to the Kourion belt is an 8th century bronze ornament from the necropolis of Salamis in eastern Cyprus. On this piece, the lions, held aloft by the nude figure of Ishtar, are attacked by what appear to be winged griffins (Karageorghis 1973b:85, pl. CCLXXII). Other griffin-lion combats from this period are very rare. An ivory plaque from Samos, dated by its context to the middle third of the 7th century, is engraved with a griffin in the act of clawing a crouching lion (Vierneisel and Walter 1959:40, pl. 86). Another ivory, from 9th century Nimrud, shows lions, bulls, and griffins in continuous combat (Mallowan 1966:534, 535, no. 452). Finally, a possible example is to be found among other ivories excavated at Nimrud (Barnett 1975:72, 195-196, no. S. 62, pl. XXXVI).

While the rarity of combats between lions and griffins makes it impossible to trace an even development and place the belt from Kourion at any specific point, lion combats with a bull or a stag as victim are extremely common in the Near East and were enthusiastically adopted into Greek art during the Orientalizing period. A horse blinker from Salamis, discovered in the same tomb as the bronze ornament mentioned previously, illustrates this type of combat. Like the bronze belt fragments from Kourion, the blinker is executed in repoussé with chased details (Karageorghis 1973b: pls. LXXXVI, CCLXVII, no. 183). The two lines used to indicate the musculature of the lion's hind leg are similar to those of the griffin on the Kourion belt and show the same stylization borrowed by Greek vase painters. A similar technique and theme are seen on 8th to 7th century Assyrian plaques, where a variation of the standard lion combat shows a lion and a lioness stalking a caprid (Parrot 1958:172, pls. XIII, XIV). Although these pieces do not relate to the Kourion belt in their style, which is purely Assyrian, they do demonstrate the predilection for balanced combats.

The row of stylized date palms in the background of the Kourion belt has a long history in Eastern art (Danthine 1937:86). It is characteristic, for example, of Assyrian works. One panel of the obelisk of Shalmaneser III shows a lion attacking a stag with the typical palms as a backdrop (Frankfort 1970:167, no. 193). Although the obelisk dates to the 9th century, the same conventional use of palm trees was still extensively utilized for the bas reliefs in the North Palace of the 7th century Assyrian king Ashurbanipal (Albenda 1976:69, fig. 18). As is so often the case, this motif was adopted into the Phoenician repertoire. A drawing showing the decoration of a silver cauldron discovered in Etruria illustrates what may be a Phoenician or Cypriote use of palms (Curtis 1919: pl. 16). Poulsen (1912:25) classifies this cauldron from the Bernardini **tomb as** Phoenician, as does Brown, who dates it to the 7th century (1960:29). Pallottino terms this piece "Cypro-Phoenician" (1975:275). Similarly decorated metalwork, usually in the form of bowls, has been found mainly in Etruria and Cyprus. Frankfort notes that, while Etruscan contexts suggest an early 7th century date, those bowls found on Cyprus may be later (1970:199).

The lion in the center of the cauldron from the Bernardini tomb has a small spiral springing from the outline of the mane. A variation of this feature appears on the lion on the right side of the Kourion belt, where the outline of the mane forms a small volute over the shoulder (Figures 8-1, 8-2). This very distinctive stylization first appears on a limestone proto-Cypriote lion (Myres 1914: no. 1393; Yon 1973:33, fig. 14) and is a common feature of small limestone ex-voto lions found at various sites on Cyprus (Yon 1973:21, fig. 10; pl. 6b, 8c) (Figure 8-3). Other lions with this same detail have been found on Samos (Schmidt 1968: pl. 115), on Rhodes (Blinkenberg 1931:404, 454-455, pl. 77, nos. 1825, 1832, 1833), and at Naukratis (Gardner 1888:58, pl. XIV, 6 [not 7]). Examples discovered outside Cyprus have been recognized as Cypriote products.

A fragment of a large terracotta figurine discovered at Kazaphani, Cyprus, and clearly produced locally belongs to the Cypro-Archaic period, 600-475 B.C. (Karageorghis 1978b:191, pl. XLVII). On one decorative register, a stamp of a man stabbing a lion with a sword has been impressed at regular intervals (Figure 8-4). In this example, the lion also has a voluted mane. Since the design is in low relief, the lion on the terracotta figurine provides an especially fine parallel for that on the Kourion belt.

The source of the voluted mane is uncertain. Yon (1973:39) states that the volutes on the manes of the limestone votive lions represent an elaboration of the simple, pointed outline of the manes on representations of Egyptian lions. Indeed, the lion in the center of the Bernardini cauldron (Curtis 1919: pl. 16) has much in common with the Egyptian lion from Dier el-Bahari illustrated by Yon (1973: pl. 12b). The shape of the head, the graceful, slender body, and the outline of the mane, aside from the spiral, are all very similar. The iconography of a lion standing over its crawling human victim is also Egyptian (Bisi 1962:230-232).

Less likely, perhaps, is the possibility that the voluted design was adopted from neo-Hittite lions such as those at Ain Dara, dated to the Late Hittite I period, ca. 2000-950 B.C. (Orthmann 1971: pls. I, A/a; 2, Ba/2). Payne (1931:16) comments that "...early Cretan and Cypriote lions are unquestionably based on Hittite originals." Depictions of lions judged to be neo-Hittite have been found on Cyprus, and it has even been suggested that a neo-Hittite community existed in the area of the Karpas Peninsula during the 9th century (Ussishkin 1972:304-305). Voluted manes such as those on the lions from Ain Dara, however, are not typical of neo-Hittite lions.

The Amathus shield boss, made of bronze with a central spike, a cable pattern band, and a register of bull and lion combats in relief, was recently the subject of an investigation by Barnett (1977). A bowl discovered in the same tomb has obvious Phoenician affinities. In spite of the fact that the boss is decorated in a style "utterly different" from that of the bowl, Barnett holds that Phoenician workshops located on Cyprus were probably responsible for producing the shield boss and other metalwork found on Cyprus. The lions on the boss (ibid.:161, fig. 1) exhibit a voluted mane similar to others previously discussed.

Might not the volute be a specifically Cypriote innovation, developed from the outline of the manes of Egyptian lions, as employed in Phoenician art? The voluted mane appears on Cypriote sculpture in the last years of the 7th century B.C., becoming widespread during the first half of the 6th century, the period of the limestone ex-voto lions (Yon 1973:19, 41-42) (Figure 8-3) and the hollow terracotta figurine with stamped decoration (Karageorghis 1978b:191) (Figure 8-4). The presence of the volute on the lion's mane on the Kourion belt makes it most likely that the belt is of Cypriote manufacture. On the basis of the date of the votive lions and the terracotta, it can be concluded that the belt was produced during the first half of the 6th, or possibly during the last years of the 7th century B.C. The Kourion belt provides yet another example of the Cypriote talent for skillfully blending various artistic influences. While the individual motifs can be traced more or less successfully, it should be stressed that this belt is an extraordinary example of its kind, and is on the whole unparalleled.

ACKNOWLEDGMENTS

I would like to express my gratitude to Professor David Soren of the University of Missouri-Columbia and Dr. Diana Buitron of The Walters Art Gallery for permission to do research on the Kourion belt. The opportunity to work with this piece first hand was afforded by Dr. Vassos Karageorghis, who generously allowed the fragments to travel to the United States.

8-1. Bronze belt from the Sanctuary of Apollo
Hylates, Kourion (Kourion Museum BZ 4). Photo
by John Huffstot.

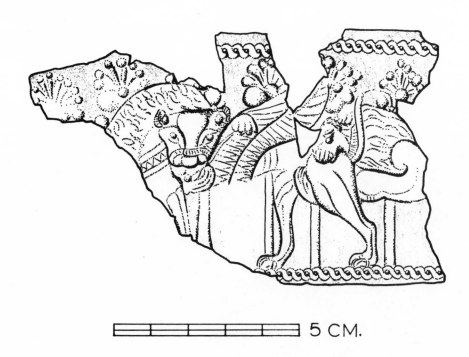

5 CM.

8-2. Bronze belt from Kourion reproduced actual
size. Drawn by John Huffstot.

8-3. Limestone ex-voto lion from Salamis, inv. no. 1788. Published by permission of the Director of Antiquities and the Cyprus Museum.

8-4. Fragment of a large terracotta figurine from Kazaphani. Published by permission of the Director of Antiquities and the Cyprus Museum.

CHAPTER 9.

A CYPRIOTE CUBICAL STAMP-SEAL

Michael Arwe

Very few examples of six-sided cubical stamp-seals exist, but one such seal was discovered within the Sanctuary of Apollo Hylates at Kourion during excavations at that site in 1947 (Figures 9-1 and 9-2). Although its archaeological context provides little information for dating, it can be attributed to the second half of the 6th century B.C. in the Cypro-Archaic period, both iconographically and on the basis of its figural quality. The seal, carved from steatite, is decorated on all six sides by intaglio carving. It is pierced through the top, allowing it to be suspended from one's wrist or neck. While the base may actually have been used as an identifiable seal, the other sides were most likely only decorative and may have served an apotropaic function. The character of this seal-stone, not only in terms of its shape, but especially in relation to the decorative motives employed, makes it an important piece of the Cypro-Archaic period.

To understand Cyprus during this era, one must first have some knowledge of the political events which influenced the island. In 709 B.C. the kings of Cyprus submitted to Sargon II of Assyria, and this Assyrian domination lasted 40 years. Although Cyprus was politically and economically controlled at this time, culturally, however, this was a time of great growth, especially because of expanding con-nections with other parts of the Near Eastern world. In fact, with the end of this period of political domination, there came an era of independence which further increased Cyprus' cultural activity. The Mycenaean Greek traditions of the past were replaced by a strong oriental influence, which involved various Egyptian, Phoenician, Syrian, and Anatolian elements (Gjerstad 1948:452). This Mixed Oriental Style, incorporating an eclectic Near Eastern art as well as Archaic Greek developments, resulted in the type of archaic art represented on the Kourion stamp-seal.

The cubical shape of the stamp-seal is quite uncommon, and the beveled edges of the top section are unique. The only multisided seals in the Mediterranean during the second millennium seem to have been the "hammer" type Hittite stamps, with decorative carving on the four sides and bottom (Bielinski 1974:59). With the beginning of the first millennium, however, variations of these shapes became more widely used. Pierced cubical "dice" and cubical shapes with handles began to appear in North Syria and Cyprus, such as a piece dating to the 8th century B.C. (Bielinski 1974: fig. 1) and another of the 7th century (Culican 1977: pl. XVII, B). In this period, stamp-seals, long a tradition on Cyprus, regained their popularity in the Near East and were never again superseded by the cylinders of Mesopotamia.

The first millennium also marked the transition to a more decorative use of stamps. On the basis of stylistic parallels, Bielinski has concluded that these six-sided forms, while developed from the Hittite "hammer," were most likely a Syrian or Phoenician innovation (Bielinski 1974:66). Not only was this area "the common melting-pot of the various artistic traditions of the time" (ibid.), but Cyprus, as well as almost all other areas with cubical seals, had close Syrian connections during the first half of the first millennium. The Kourion seal, then, is a Cypriote product of this Syro-Phoenician school of cubical and conical shapes which had taken on a predominantly ornamental function.

The shape of the Kourion seal is not the only product of the strong Near Eastern influence on Cyprus. The iconography of the piece has its origin in the Mixed Oriental Style as well. The four main panels of the seal show, respectively, a man holding a branch, a hawk or eagle, a grotesque horned figure, and a striding warrior (Figure 9-2). Various other elements are shown above and below, such as two grotesque heads, cocks, a crab, ducks, and some sort of design or symbol, probably a mark of identification, especially considering its position on the bottom surface.

The first panel can be interpreted as a single figure in a Near Eastern sacred tree worship scene. Although more commonly shown with two figures, one on either side of the tree such as on an earlier Cypriote cylinder seal (Ohnefalsch-Richter 1893: fig. 131), it was not unusual for a single figure to be shown. In fact, the single figure was not uncommon on Neo-Assyrian and Syrian glyptics of this period (Bielinski 1974:57).

The second panel shows a hawk in a frontal, spread-wing pose, and, although no parallel has been found for this depiction, it probably derives from some Egyptian form, perhaps relating to the god Horus.

The third panel illustrates the clearest indication of the Mixed Oriental Style. Shown is the Egyptian dwarf god Bes surrounded by vegetal elements which probably reflect the sacred tree worship of the first panel. This Bes, however, is a perfect example of the mixture of orientalizing styles found during this period. Although at first glance the protruding tongue suggests the figure's identification as a Gorgon, a contemporary relief from Cyprus, identified by Wilson as a Bes-mask (1975:100), which also parallels the heads on the top and bottom panels of the seal, and a 7th century bronze figurine from Nimrud (Oates 1959: pl. XXXI) show that this is a characteristic common to the Egyptian god as well. The position of Bes' arms bent over his chect in this manner is also most probably part of the god's Phonician iconography and, in fact, other examples indicate that it was particularly popular on the island of Cyprus (Wilson 1975:86). Other variations in the god's appearance also point to Eastern influences. The fact that Bes is shown as a full-sized figure is another Phoenician variation of his Egyptian form and is paralleled on a Cypriote sarcophagus in the Metropolitan Museum from the second half of the 6th century B.C. (Myres 1914:232, no. 1365D). While generally shown naked in Egyptian art, Bes on the Kourion seal appears to be dressed in the open kilt which he quite commonly wears in Near Eastern depictions. Finally, Bes is represented with two short horns, a characteristic also paralleled in the sarcophagus relief in the Metropolitan Museum. While theories concerning the origin of these horns vary from influences of the Babylonian god Humbaba (Wilson 1975:97) to the Greek Pan (Culican 1968:95), their presence on this piece removes any doubt as to its provenience, since horned Bes figures are virtually unknown anywhere by the island of Cyprus.

Finally, the last panel illustrates the only true Greek scene, that of a striding Greek warrior with characteristic shield and crested helmet. While the Mixed Oriental Style did dominate in Cyprus at this time, artistic developments in archaic Greece were also being felt, as seen from this fourth panel as well as the upper relief of an early 5th century sarcophagus from Cyprus (Myres 1914:229, no. 1364A).

Thus, both in light of its unusual cubical shape, originating in the Syrian school of stamps, as well as the eclectic artistic influences of Egypt, Phoenicia, and Greece which formed its decoration, this stamp-seal from the Sanctuary of Apollo at Kourion is an important piece in furthering our understanding of the cultural identity of archaic Cyprus.

9-1. Steatite stamp-seal
from the Sanctuary of
Apollo Hylates at Kourion
(Kourion Museum St. 846).
Photo by John Huffstot.

9-2. Stamp-seal. Drawn by John Huffstot.

CHAPTER 10

THE CULTS OF APOLLO IN CYPRUS: A PRELIMINARY SURVEY

Stephen C. Glover

On Cyprus, Apollo ranks second only to Aphrodite in the number of dedications and sanctuaries. These dedications attest to the wide distribution and variety of Apollo cults, and the diverse origins and cultural influences reflected in the cult epithets document the interaction of Cypriote, Greek, and Phoenician religious traditions. The cults of Apollo in Cyprus provide further evidence of the island's cultural complexity.

Apollo Hylates, Apollo of the Woodland, is the best known of the individual cults because of the continuing excavations of the sanctuary at Kourion (Figure 10-1). A second sanctuary of Apollo Hylates is located in the eastern necropolis of Nea Paphos (Figure 10-1). Resembling a tomb, the sanctuary consists of a dromos and two subterranean chambers carved from bedrock. The first chamber is rectangular, with semicircular niches set into two of its walls. The second chamber is circular, with a domed roof pierced by an "oculus" at a point slightly off center. Two Cypro-syllabic inscriptions are carved into the rock, the first above the entrance to the sanctuary, and the second on a wall of the first chamber. Dated to the late 4th century B.C., the inscriptions are nearly identical in content. They record the construction of the sanctuary for Apollo Hylates by a high priest (Masson 1961: 96-99, nos. 2,3). Unfortunately, the poor preservation of portions of the texts has obscured the name of the priest, which was either Τάρβας (Deecke 1886: 319; Masson 1961: 98) or Σατράπας (Mitford 1960a: 5,6).

In addition to the cult centers at Kourion and Nea Paphos, inscriptions attest to the presence of sanctuaries of Apollo Hylates at Dhrymou and Chytroi. The evidence for a sanctuary at Dhrymou (Figure 10-1) rests on two Cypro-syllabic inscriptions found in 1868 or 1869 by a shepherd at a site approximately 1 mile north of the village, not far from the ruined church of Ayios Minas (Masson 1961: 138-139). In 1888, D.G. Hogarth visited Dhrymou and questioned the villagers about the site of the discoveries (Hogarth 1889:30-31). He was told that Besh-Besh, the foreman of Luigi Palma di Cesnola, had dug at the site and had found terracottas and statuettes. However, Cesnola does not mention these excavations in his book

Cyprus: its Ancient Cities, Tombs and Temples(1877). Intriguingly, Hogarth reported finding two rudely shaped conical blocks near the church. The larger of these two blocks was 4 feet high, with two holes near the apex. The other block had a single perforation. Large conical blocks, usually with a single perforation, have been reported at Kouklia (ancient Paphos) and at sites in every region of Cyprus (Hogarth 1889:46-48). These conical stones may have been baetyls, sacred stones. Small, conical but solid, baetyls have been discovered at the Sanctuary of Apollo Hylates at Kourion (Buitron and Soren 1979:26-27). An ashlar block with a roughly rectangular perforation also was found at Kourion near the Archaic Altar. Originally published as a fence post for a low barrier surrounding the altar (Scranton 1967:7, fig. 2c), the block is now believed to be a baetyl (Buitron and Soren 1979:22 and this volume).[1] Thus, the blocks found by Hogarth may have been baetyls associated with a sanctuary of Apollo Hylates in the vicinity of the church of Ayios Minas. Although the site has long been acknowledged as the probable location of a sanctuary of Apollo Hylates (Hogarth 1889: 31; Masson 1961:139, note 6), systematic excavations have not yet been undertaken.

The inscriptions from Dhrymou are of particular interest for the dedicatory formulas they employ, since only the epithet Hylates is given. The first inscription records a dedication made τῶι θεῶι Ὑλάται, to the god of the Woodland, by Onasiwoikos, son of Stasiwoikos. The second inscription is dedicated τῷ Ὑλάται to "Him of the Woodland," by Aristophantos, son of Aristagoras (Masson 1961: 141-142, nos. 85, 86).

Two Cypro-syllabic inscriptions found at Chytroi also employ only the epithet Hylates. The site of ancient Chytroi is located approximately 1 mile to the east of the modern village of Kythrea on a hill occupied by the ruins of Ayios Dhimitrianos (Figure 10-1). The two inscriptions of Hylates were found on the hill of Skali to the northwest of Ayios Dhimitrianos (Masson 1961: 258-259, 264-265). The first inscription, incised on a small bronze cup, was found in 1910 by Stavros Oikonomides, an inhabitant of Kythrea (Peristianes 1910: 862). The text of the inscription simply stated that the cup was τῶ θεῶ Ὑλάταυ, of the god of the Woodland, i.e., the property of the god (Masson 1961: 264-265, no. 250). The second inscription, incised on a flat-bottomed clay bowl, was found in a well in association with Hellenistic sherds, dating to ca. 300 B.C., and with fragments of large terracotta bulls. The text identifies the bowl as τῶ Ὑλάτω, of "Him of the Woodland" (Karageorghis 1960: 260-261, fig. 29; Masson 1961: 265, no. 250a).[2] Masson (1961:264) strongly urged that an excavation be conducted at Chytroi-Skali, since it would probably reveal a sanctuary of Apollo Hylates. As of this date, however, such excavations have not taken place.

In addition to the ancient sites of Kourion, Nea Paphos, and Chytroi, and the modern village of Dhrymou, there were sancturies of Apollo Hylates at Amamassos, Erystheia, and Tembros, but these are known only from the list given by Stephanos of Byzantium (*Ethnika*, s.v.Ἐρύσθεια). In 1890, A.A. Sakellarios (1890:136) suggested that Tempria, near ancient Soli (Figure 10-1), was the site of ancient Tembros, and the modern village of Dhrymou may be the location of another site listed by Stephanos, since the ancient name of Dhrymou is unknown. None of the towns named by Stephanos, however, has been verified and located by inscriptions.

Apollo Hylates also appears in Egypt where he is named, along with Leto, Artemis, and Herakles, in a dedication from Koptos by Apollonios, the διοκητής, or chief financial officer of Ptolemy Philadelphos (283-245 B.C.), (Milne 1901: 290-291, no. 11; Fraser 1972: 1, 195-196). In addition, Pausanias (10.32.6) mentions a cult of Apollo at a place called Ὕλαι near Magnesia-on-the-Maeander. The cult image, located in a cave, inspired worshippers to uproot and carry trees.

Apollo Hylates seems to have been regarded, however, as a preeminently Cypriote divinity in antiquity. The Hellenistic poet Lycophron termed Cyprus the "land of Hylates" (*Alexandra* 448). In the early Roman imperial period, the indigenous character of the cult is underscored in an inscription recording the Cypriote oath of allegiance to Tiberius in 14 A.D. Found in 1959 at Nikoklia near Kouklia, the inscription lists Apollo Hylates as one of several divinities invoked as ἡμέτερος, "our own," by which the inhabitants of Cyprus pledge their loyalty to the new emperor (Mitford 1960b: 75–79).

Originally, Apollo Hylates was probably a local woodland deity assimilated to Apollo in the 5th century B.C., the date of the earliest dedication to Apollo in the sanctuary at Kourion (Mitford 1971: 46–49, no. 18). Dedications of the 7th and 6th centuries B.C. at Kourion simply refer to "the god." The inscriptions at Dhrymou and Chytroi which refer solely to Hylates may reflect a more conservative religious tradition in which the cult retained its original form.

Another cult named in the oath of allegiance to Tiberius is Apollo Kerynetes, Apollo of Keryneia, the modern Kyrenia (Figure 10-1).[3] Known only from the Cypriote oath of allegiance, the epithet Kerynetes suggests the assimilation of the civic god of Keryneia to Apollo. A cult recognized throughout the island appears to have undergone the same process of assimilation as indicated by a dedication to Apollo Kyprios found in the vicinity of ancient Soli; the inscription dates to the 3rd century B.C. (Mitford 1961: 134, no. 34).

An altar discovered by D.G. Hogarth at Marathounda near Nea Paphos (Figure 10-1) bears another epithet of Apollo related to sacred trees, Apollo Myrtates, Apollo of the Myrtle, in a dedication of the late Hellenistic period (Hogarth 1889: 23–24, no. 8). Although Apollo Myrtates appears to be unique to Cyprus (Karageorghis 1965a:250), the variant form μυρτῷος does occur as an epithet of Apollo in Cyrene (Hogarth 1889:24).

The rite of sacrifice and the practice of divination appear to have been linked intimately in a sanctuary of Apollo excavated by the British consul R.H. Lang in 1868 at Pyla northeast of Larnaca (Figure 10-1). Lang found six inscriptions, two in Cypro-syllabic and four in alphabetic Greek (Colonna-Ceccaldi 1882: 20–22, 198–200; Besques 1936:3–11; Masson 1966:11–21). The alphabetic inscriptions have been dated to the Hellenistic period (Besques 1936:4); the two Cypro-syllabic inscriptions have not been closely dated, but probably date to the 5th or 4th century B.C. One of the inscriptions records a simple dedication to Apollo, while four record dedications to Apollo Magirios (or Mageirios in one of the texts). The epithet derives from μάγειρος meaning butcher or cook. The μάγειροι of a sanctuary were the sacred butchers, those who perfomed the sacrifices in the temple. Μάγειροι are widely attested in inscriptions from Greece, Asia Minor, and Syria, but Pyla appears to be the sole instance of the dedication of a sanctuary to Apollo as patron of the sacrificers (Besques 1936:6–7). The sixth inscription, one of the four in alphabetic Greek, is dedicated to Apollo Lakeutes by a μαντίαρχος, a chief of diviners. The epithet Λακευτής may be related to the verbs λάσκω (to crackle, cry, make resound), λακάζω (to cry), and λακέω (to crackle). The derivative epithet Λακευτής would then signify that which makes Apollo's voice resound, i.e., the crackling and popping of flesh burning on the altar (Masson 1960a:112–114; Robert 1978:338–344). This particular oracular cult of Apollo appears to be unique to Cyprus.

Perhaps the most enigmatic of the cults of Apollo on Cyprus is that of Apollo Melanthios, attested in a dedication of the 3rd century B.C. from a sanctuary at Amargetti in the foothills of the Troodos Mountains northeast of Nea Paphos (Figure 10-1).

Excavated in 1888 by Hogarth (1888: 171-174), the sanctuary yielded nine dedications to an Opaon Melanthios and a single dedication to Apollo Melanthios (Gardner et al. 1888: 261-262). Opaon Melanthios appears to have been a local fertility deity (Mitford 1946: 39; Mitford 1961: 136) assimilated to Apollo in the 3rd century B.C.

In several bilingual Phoenician/Cypro-syllabic inscriptions, Apollo is equated with the Phoenician deity Reshef. The earliest of these, dating to 388 B.C., was found in a sanctuary excavated by R.H. Lang in 1869 at Idalion, the modern Dhali (Figure 10-1) (1878: 30-71; Masson 1968: 386-402). The Phoenician text records the dedication of a statuette to Reshef Mikal by Baalrom, son of Abdmilk. In the Cypro-syllabic text, Reshef Mikal is translated as Apollo Amyklos. Amyklos seems to be a phonetic rendering of the Phoenician Mikal, rather than an importation of the Laconian cult of Apollo at Amyklai (Masson 1960b: 138-139; 1961: 246-248, no. 220). This would appear to be confirmed by a dedication of the early 3rd century B.C. from Larnaca, the site of ancient Kition. The inscription records the offering of a sacrifice to Apollo Mikal by Pyntokla, the daughter of Philoitos (Nicolaou 1969: 87-90, no. 16). To the Greek dedicant, who seems to have been unaware of the Hellenized form Amyklos, the cult remained essentially Semitic and distinct from the Laconian cult of Apollo. Nevertheless, both Reshef and Apollo at Amyklai were warrior gods (Conrad 1971: 172-173; Martin 1976: 205-218), suggesting that the equation of the two deities was based on more than phonetics.

Two similar bilingual dedications were found in a sanctuary excavated in 1885 by Ohnefalsch-Richter in the valley of Phrangissa near the ancient site of Tamassos (Figure 10-1) (1893: 6-10). In the first, dating to 362 B.C., a statuette is dedicated to Reshef 'lyyt by Menahem in the Phoenician text. In the Cypro-syllabic text, Reshef 'lyyt is translated as Apollo Heleitas. The Greek epithet may derive from a local toponym, Helos, while the Phoenician 'lyyt appears to be a transcription of Heleitas minus the aspirant (Masson 1960b:139; 1961: 224-226, no. 215). The second bilingual, dating to 375 B.C., records the dedication by Abdsasom of a statuette to Reshef 'lhyts, translated as Apollo Alasiotas in the Greek text. As in the first bilingual, the Phoenician epithet is a transcription of the Greek epithet. Alasiotas is the ethnic of Alasia, which is generally believed to be the Bronze Age name of Cyprus (Masson 1960b: 139-141; 1961: 226-228, no. 216).[4] The epithet Alasiotas suggests the persistence of a Cypriote religious tradition that extends back to the Bronze Age.

The Tamassos-Phrangissa bilingual inscriptions date before the annexation of Tamassos by the kingdom of Kition, which occurred between 361 and 351 B.C. (Gjerstad 1948: 497). Thus, the Phoenicians made their dedications in a Greek Cypriote milieu to distinctively Cypriote divinities who had been assimilated to Apollo and, in turn, identified their own god Reshef with the Cypriote forms of Apollo.

In addition to the Cypriote cults assimilated to Apollo, several Apollo cults appear to be importations. Apollo Pythios, the Apollo of Delphi, is attested in a dedication of ca. 221-205 B.C. in the Sanctuary of Apollo Hylates at Kourion (Mitford 1971: 89-91, no. 41). Apollo Lyk(e)ios, Apollo the "wolf god" or "Lycian Apollo" (Miller 1939: 5-7, 36-37; Guthrie 1951: 82-84), is attested in an early 3rd century B.C. dedication found in a sanctuary excavated by the Swedish Cyprus Expedition at Mersinaki near ancient Soli (Gjerstad et al. 1937: 622, no. 4). Pausanias lists three cult centers of Apollo Lykeios on the Greek mainland: Athens (1. 19. 3), Sikyon (2. 9. 7), and Argos (2. 19. 3). An inscription of the late 3rd or early 2nd century B.C. found at Vigla near Dhekelia (Figure 10-1) is dedicated to Apollo Keraiates

(Mitford 1961: 116, no. 16). Keraiates, "He of the Horn," is a Cypriote variant of Kereates, an epithet of Apollo in southern Arcadia (Pausanias 8. 34. 5). A Cypro-syllabic inscription discovered at Lefkoniko, northwest of ancient Salamis, records the name of Apollo Dauchnaphorios (Masson 1961: 311-312, no. 309). Dauchnaphorios is the Cypriote dialectal form of Daphnephoros, the epithet of Apollo at Thebes (Pausanias 9. 10. 4) and Eretria (*IG* 12, 9, 210). Daphnephoros refers to the legendary first temple of Apollo at Delphi, said to have been built of bay branches brought by the god himself from the Vale of Tempe (Pausanias 10. 5. 9). Finally, an inscription from the vicinity of Kythrea records a dedication to Apollo Agy(i)ates (Menardos 1906: 334-335). Agyiates is a synonym for Agyieus, an epithet of Apollo signifying the god as guardian of streets and highways. The cult is attested at Acharnai, Athens, Argos, Tegea, Megalopolis, Corcyra, Thera, and Halikarnassos (Cook 1925: 163-164; Miller 1939: 46). The cult image was a stone pillar placed at the entryway of a house on the street (Miller 1939: 46-47). The pillar of Apollo Agyieus parallels the baetyls associated with the cult of Apollo Hylates at Kourion (supra p. 144).

Although several Apollo sanctuaries, such as that of Apollo Hylates at Kourion, were active in the Cypro-Archaic period (ca. 750-475 B.C.), Apollo's name does not appear in the dedications until the succeeding period. The emergence of Apollo cults in Cyprus appears to coincide with the reestablishment of close cultural ties with the Greek mainland in the second half of the 5th century B.C. Spurred by the pro-Athenian policy of Evagoras I of Salamis (411 to 374/73 B.C.), Cyprus underwent a process of Hellenization that continued throughout the 4th century, despite the maintenance of Persian control until 332 B.C. (Gjerstad 1948: 502-505). The assimilation of Cypriote and Phoenician cults to Apollo, along with the importation of Apollo cults from mainland Greece and the Aegean, mark the religious aspect of Hellenization, a process that culminated under Ptolemaic rule (294-58 B.C.).

Such epithets as Alasiotas, on the other hand, indicate that indigenous traditions persisted to a remarkable degree. The designation of Apollo Hylates and Apollo Kerynetes as ἡμέτερος in the oath of allegiance to Tiberius suggests that, while these cults were assimilated to Hellenic Apollo, they retained distinctively Cypriote features.

The Cypro-Classical and Hellenistic periods have generally received less attention than earlier eras of Cypriote civilization, yet the processes of assimilation and importation reflected in the development of Apollo cults indicate that these were periods of dynamic cultural change on the island. Cyprus joined the larger Greek world, rediscovering her Hellenic heritage, while at the same time retaining elements of her culture which were uniquely her own.

NOTES

1. Aniconic imagery also played a prominent role in the cult of Aphrodite at Palaeopaphos. A baetyl forms the centerpiece of Roman coin images of the sanctuary of Aphrodite (Westholm 1933: 201-236; Maier 1975: 70-71).

2. According to Masson (1961: 265), the genitive ῾Υλάτω in the second inscription, in place of ῾Υλάται, reflects the influence of the κοινή genitive form, ῾Υλάτου.

3.   The other deities characterized as ἡμέτεροι are Aphrodite Akraia (Aphrodite of the Headland), the "saving Dioscouroi," and Kore. A sanctuary of Aphrodite Akraia at the tip of the Karpas Peninsula is mentioned by Strabo (14.682). The Dioskouroi and Kore, in this context, may represent assimilated local deities.

4.   For a recent examination of the documentary and archaeological evidence for the identification of Alasia with Cyprus, see Hellbing (1979).

ACKNOWLEDGMENTS

I would like to express my gratitude to Dr. Vassos Karageorghis for his assistance and encouragement, and to Professors David Soren and Eugene Lane of the University of Missouri-Columbia for their comments and criticisms.

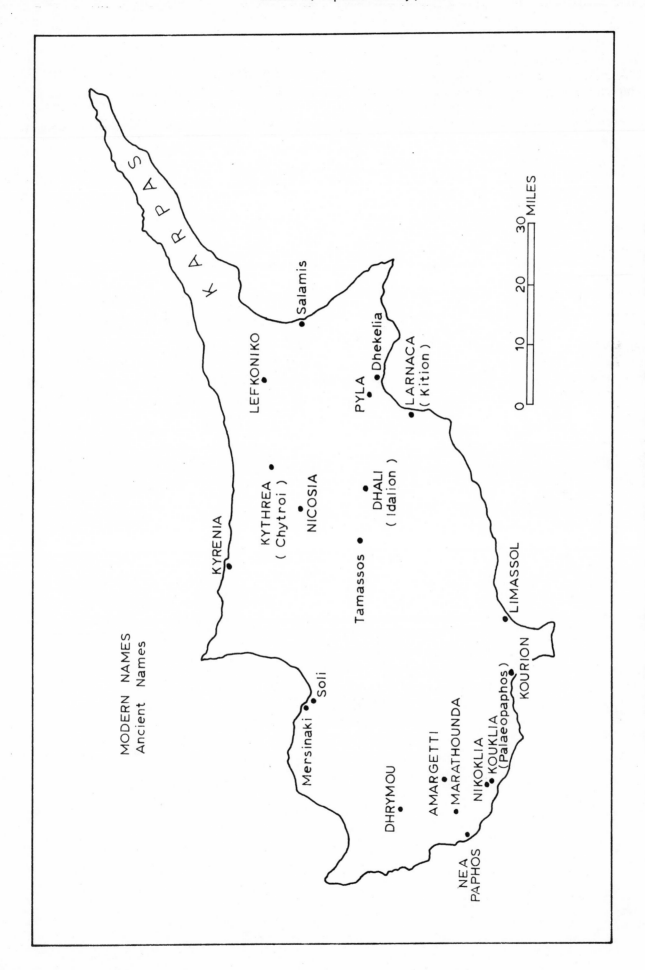

10-1. Map of Cyprus showing Apollo sanctuary sites. Drawn by John Huffstot.

CHAPTER 11.

Ἄλσος AND THE SANCTUARY OF APOLLO HYLATES

Darice Birge

Recent excavations at the sanctuary of Apollo Hylates at Kourion revealed evidence of a stand of sacred trees planted within a monumental walkway or enclosure. This new physical information may be supported by an ancient source: Aelian, writing in the 2nd or 3rd century A.D., mentions a sacred grove at Kourion in his work on marvellous occurrences in nature. This combination of archaeological and literary evidence invites consideration of the ancient Greek term for a sacred grove, ἄλσος, as it applies to the sanctuary of a god of nature at Kourion.

In the Greek world in general, the word ἄλσος underwent a transformation through the course of antiquity that recalls two processes of definition in religion which occur on physical and theological levels. Marked boundaries distinguish sacred territory, and monumental altars and temples emphasize its holiness. Naming an aspect of the divine in nature and providing descriptive epithets distinguish a god thus derived from other deities. At the sanctuary of Apollo Hylates ("of the woodlands"), these processes perhaps reflect an increasing separation of humans from nature. The same phenomenon of detachment can be observed in the evolution of the word ἄλσος.

First, a brief summary of the Kourion sanctuary's growth and the development of the deity worshipped there is in order. The excavations of the sanctuary, conducted principally by the University of Missouri-Columbia and The Walters Art Gallery, are providing new information about the mature stage of a long established religious center on the southwest coast of Cyprus. The 1st century Temple of Apollo and the roughly contemporary tree planting pits and circular walkway (Tholos) to the west of the paved street dividing the sanctuary (as well as the earlier excavated Northwest and Southeast Buildings) (Figure 11-1) were constructed when the cult of Apollo Hylates reached its zenith at Kourion. The earliest securely known remains of worship on the site are figurines and pottery dating to the late 7th century B.C. From the designation of a particularly sacred area, presumably at about this time, to "an elaborate scheme for attracting and entertaining visitors" in the time of Trajan (Scranton 1967: 6, 71-74), the architectural development finds a parallel in the progressive clarification of the deity worshipped at Kourion.

Epigraphical evidence from the site shows the gradual transformation of the god from an undefined deity to Apollo Hylates. For example, a Corinthian vase (oinochoe) from the later 6th century and an Egyptian bronze situla from the 26th dynasty bear dedications in the Cypriote syllabary to "the god" (Mitford 1971: 38-42, nos. 14, 15; Masson 1961: 199, nos. 188, 189). This divinity is named for the first time as Apollo on a "temple-boy" statuette dated on epigraphical grounds to the 5th century (Mitford 1971: 46-49, no. 18; Masson 1961: 198, no. 184). Only in the 3rd century B.C. is the god first called Apollo Hylates in a dedication possibly by Antiochos of Epiros, son of Nikanor (Mitford 1971: 119-122, no. 60).

Late sources tell of the worship of Apollo Hylates at Kourion. The lexicographer Stephanos of Byzantium (s.v. ῞Υλη) reports ῞Υλη: πόλις Κύπρου ἐν ᾗ ᾿Απόλλων τιμᾶται ῾Υλάτης (Hyle, a city of Cyprus, in which Apollo Hylates is honored), and Tzetzes (*ad Lyc.* 448) comments: ῞Υλη γάρ ἐστι περὶ τὸ Κούριον, τόπον τῆς Κύπρου, ἱερὰ ᾿Απόλλωνος ἀφ᾿ ῆς ῾Υλάτην τὸν θεὸν προσαγορεύουσιν(for near Kourion, a place in Cyprus, is Hyle, sacred to Apollo, whence they call the god Hylates). The ethnic term Hylates tells nothing about the specific character of the deity. As a place name, however, Hyle suggests that the area was wooded and distinguished from more open surrounding land. Aelian's account (*On The Characteristics Of Animals 11.7*) describes an unusual feature of the Apollo Hylates sanctuary – its wooded "game preserve."

᾿Εν Κουριάδι αἱ ἔλαφοι (πλῆθος δὲ ἄρα τούτων τῶν θηρίων ἐνταῦθά ἐστι, καὶ πολλοὶ θηραταὶ περὶ τὴν ἄγραν αὐτῶν ἠνέμωνται) ὅταν καταφύγωσιν ἐς τὸ τοῦ ᾿Απόλλωνος ἱερὸν τὸ ἐνταυθοῖ (ἔστι δὲ ἄλσος μέγιστον) ὑλακτοῦσι μὲν οἱ κύνες, πλησίον δὲ ἐλθεῖν οὐχ ὑπομένουσιν· αἱ δὲ συστᾶσαι νέμονται ἄτρεπτον καὶ ἀδεᾶ τὴν νομήν, ἀπορρήτῳ τινὶ φύσει τὴν ὑπὲρ ἑαυτῶν σωτηρίαν τῷ θεῷ πιστεύουσαι αἱ ἔλαφοι.

At Kourias the deer (there are a great number of these animals here, and many hunters eager to pursue them), when they flee hither for refuge, to the sanctuary of Apollo (which includes a very large grove), the dogs bay at them but do not dare to come close. The herds graze unperturbed and fearlessly; by some mysterious natural instinct the deer trust in the god for their safety [translation adapted from Scholfield, *Aelian* 1959].

Worship in a wooded area and protection of animals show the concern of Apollo Hylates with nature.

The planting pits for trees in the western enclosure demonstrate both the god's concern with nature and human alteration of the natural site. Apparently, in the 1st century after Christ, trees were planted intentionally for religious or environmental reasons in an area presumably named for its wood, which flourished once, if not throughout its history, and possessed in Aelian's time a μέγιστον ἄλσος (very large grove).

Although the word ἄλσος had taken on new meanings before his time, Aelian uses the term in its traditional sense. Broadly speaking, an ἄλσος is a precinct containing trees, with or without associated structures, enclosed or not, and usually sacred in itself. It may be sacred in two senses: as a parcel of territory in an urban or rural setting and as an indefinite habitat of divine beings in the rural landscape, not ostensibly established by humans. In the course of time, the original meaning was expanded. Secular meanings were added, and the use of ἄλσος for a type of sacred territory was altered radically. On the one hand, the term ἄλσος intensifies the religious quality associated with a precinct and lends an air of holiness to a place not ordinarily sacred in itself. It also takes on new secular meanings, that of a specific natural habitat in scientific works, and a shady and refreshing nook in pastoral poetry.

A comparison of ἄλσος with the word τέμενος which also can be used to describe a sacred precinct, provides an interesting perspective from which to view sacred groves. Since the last century, etymological dictionaries have mainly derived ἄλσος from the Indo-European root *al-*, to grow or increase, which would emphasize the grove as a collection of growing trees (Curtius 1875-76: 444-445; Prellwitz 1892: s.v. ἄλσος ; Snell and Mette 1955: cols. 581-582; Pokorny 1959:26; Hofmann 1950: s.v. ; Chantrain 1968: s.v. ἄλσος). This derivation has become less popular in recent years, however. For example, Frisk prefers to leave the origin of ἄλσος unclear, and he doubts its semantic connections with "increase" (Frisk 1960: 79). Another theory, for example in Liddell and Scott's lexicon, connects the word with the Gothic *alhs*, or temple. This implies that the Indo-European root had some religious connotation before its speakers reached the Greek peninsula (Hoffmann 1899: 106; Pokorny 1959:32; Liddell and Scott 1968: s.v. ἄλσος). When comparing ἄλσος to τέμενος one finds that modern scholars for the most part connect τέμενος with τέμνω; an association which reflects a division of territory in a social, not purely religious, context, while ἄλσος emphasizes the landscape. Both terms, of course, can be used for sacred precinct.[1]

In the *Odyssey* (17. 298-299), the absent Odysseus' farmlands are called a τέμενος. ῎Οφρ᾽ ἂν ἄγοιεν/ δμῶες ᾽Οδυσσῆος τέμενος μέγα κοπρήσοντες (until the slaves could carry it away to manure the huge estate of Odysseus). The shrine of Aphrodite at Paphos is also a τέμενος, with an altar, ἐς Πάφον· ἔνθα τέ οἱ τέμενος βωμὸσ τε θυήεισ (in Paphos where her precinct and fragrant altars are (*Od*.8.363)). While τέμενοσ can refer in the *Iliad* and the *Odyssey* to the holdings of a powerful leader, ἄλσοσ, on the other hand, is used for the nymphs' habitat (*Iliad* 20.8-9, in general; *Od*. 10.350-351, Kirke's nymphs), a landmark by the shores of Ocean (*Od*. 10.508-551), and precincts of particular deities in real or imaginary towns (Ismaros/Apollo, *Od*. 9.197-201; Ithaka/Apollo, *Od*. 20.276-278; Ithaka/nymphs, *Od*. 17.205-211; Onchestos/Poseidon, *Iliad* 2.505-506; land of the Phaiakes/Athena, *Od*. 6.291-294 and 321-322). None contains any built structures except an altar of a fountain. ῎Αλσος plays an obviously sacred, and only sacred, role in urban settings and emphasizes the presence of divinity in nature as the haunt of the nymphs. Not at this stage, nor at any other time does ἄλσος ostensibly signify a privately owned or secular and civic owned stand of trees.

In the Homeric hymn to Apollo, ἄλσος is associated four times with ναός in the repeated phrase νηόν τε καὶ ἄλσεα δενδρήεντα, (a temple and a wooded grove), but this occurs only in hypothetical situations or general statements (lines 76, 143, 221, 245). When Apollo constructs a sanctuary by Telphusa's hidden stream (lines 384-385), he builds only an altar in the wooded ἄλσος. In the mythic reality expressed in the hymn, the trees of the ἄλσος exist, while the temple goes unmentioned. Apparently, the chief aspect of the ἄλσος here is its natural one, its trees, and not any built structures.[2]

A more detailed view of an ἄλσος is presented by Sappho, who appears to describe a real sanctuary with its fragrant altar and water running amid the trees (Page 1959: 34-44, fr. 2). The sanctuary also contains a temple (ibid., line 1). In this fragment, Aphrodite's grove and meadow occupy most of the poet's attention, but her inclusion of a temple reveals a new concern with man-made structures in the ἄλσος.

In the 5th century among Pindar, Bacchylides, and the tragedians, ἄλσος is expanded to include a grove whose moment of construction is known. The word is also employed metaphorically for features in both the natural and man-made environment, not necessarily associated with trees. In Pindar's third Olympian we witness planning and planting of an ἄλσος. Now ἄλσος need not be considered a parcel of land, one of whose characteristics is its existence as an ἄλσος without a specific moment of creation. Herakles lays out the Altis for Zeus with altars and a race track; it contains no trees until Herakles plants them (*Ol.* 3.16-34). Although its foundation takes place in mythic time, the ἄλσος may be planned and surveyed just as a town is. In his fifth Olympian, Pindar celebrates the settlement of Camarina. An ἄλσος of buildings makes up Psaumis' newly founded city, and the cluster of buildings is described as a cluster of trees (*Ol.* 5.10-14). Camarina, an historic town with a definite foundation, may gain some glorified existence outside ordinary time by the use of a term usually reserved for something sacred.

The metaphorical use of ἄλσος on a visual level is carried to greater abstraction through Bacchylides' and Aeschylus' expression πόντιον ἄλσος for the sea (literally, grove of the sea or the sea's domain).[3] This phrase occurs in Bacchylides 17.84-85 and in Aeschylus' *Persians* line 104. While serving to remind one of the similar sounding ἅλς (salt water), the word ἄλσος itself stands for an expanse of wild nature temporarily tamed. In both instances, a hero or a human being succeeds at a feat that ordinary folk around them would never attempt – the hitherto landlocked Persians brave the sea and build a bridge of ships, and Theseus dives into the sea to retrieve the ring of Minos and to prove through his protection that Poseidon is his father. Ἄλσος is nature, usually beyond the control of heroes or humans, which they temporarily and paradoxically dominate, thus becoming supernatural themselves.

Aeschylus uses a similar expression, ἀλίρρυτον ἄλσος (brine-washed grove), in his *Suppliant Maidens* (line 868). The Danaids are confronted by the Egyptian herald; ten lines before, the chorus wished never to look again on the nourishing waters of the Nile. Now they call for the herald to drown in the ἀλίρρυτον ἄλσος by the burial mound of Sarpedon. The close association of ἄλσος with Sarpedon's tomb reminds one of the practice of planting trees by graves. At the same time the herald would die violently, at the mercy of the all-powerful sea, plunging into untamable death without even a burial mound like Sarpedon's. This sea as ἄλσος is not nature temporarily tamable, but a destroyer, fearful and superhuman. The term helps to lend to nature the quality of a force which exists above and apart from human beings and figures of myth. That is, it may lend a sacred feeling to that which is not in itself sacred.

At the close of the century, Euripides uses ἀλσῶδες (*Iphigeneia at Aulis*, line 141), an adjectival form, to expand the use of ἄλσος in a secular sense in a context which suggests the sacred ἄλσος in the sanctuary of Artemis at Aulis. Agamemnon sends his messenger to keep Iphigeneia from her appointment as unknowing victim; while he urges the man not to fall asleep by the wooded springs along the route, he reminds one of the sacred wooded spring at Aulis in which Iphigeneia will walk to sacrifice.

In the 4th century, ἄλσος is adopted as a scientific term. Aristotle uses it to define the habitat of cicadas. They do not live in cold places; for that reason, they are not found in shady groves (*HA* 556^a.24–25). A species of eagle as well lives in plains, ἄλση, and cities (*HA* 618^b.18–20). Once again the word is used purely to describe a certain part of the natural landscape without any religious connotation.

῎Αλσος helps to set a truly secular scene in poetry in the 3rd century works of Theocritus. The worldly setting of his poem 5.31–32, with its trees, dripping water, and buzzing grasshoppers, although it need not be construed as mundane, nonetheless possesses no sacred quality. While the image the poet presents is not ordinary, it is also not supernatural. ῎Αλσος is used to help convey the ease and pleasures of an idealized but secular world.

This does not mean that ἄλσος has by now lost its original sense as a type of sanctuary. Certainly the use of ἄλσος for a wooded sacred precinct continues throughout Greek literature. Aelian uses ἄλσος in this way for the deer refuge in Apollo's sanctuary at Kourion where, nearly two centuries earlier, trees were deliberately planted in an area apparently already known for its wood. The gradual dissociation from and concurrent intervention of humankind with nature, from the time of the production of the Homeric similes to the urban and indeed cosmopolitan Hellenistic age (Hartwell 1922: 181–182), is reflected in the increased latitude of meanings for ἄλσος: first a sacred wooded precinct alone, later a metaphor for the supernatural in nature, and finally a scientific and secular application. This widened usage suggests a parallel blurring of the Greek view towards the natural landscape in religion.

NOTES

1. Compare ancient associations for τέμενος *and* ἄλσος: τέμενος τάμον *(they set apart a tract of land), Iliad 6.194 and 20.184 (not in religious contexts) and Hesychius, s.v.* ἄλσεα: τεμένη...πρὸς ἄλσιν καὶ αὔξησιν τῶν φυτῶν ὄντες ἐπιτήδειοι *(groves: "temene" . . . suitable for the growth and increase of vegetation).*

2. Note also the description of the ἄλσος of Poseidon at Onchestos in lines 229–238.

3. Commentators, for example Broadhead (1960: 55–56), note the use of πόντιον ἄλσος for the sea as holy nature.

4. See Rosenmeyer (1969: 178–205, particularly 188–190), for the grove and the landscape in Theocritus.

ACKNOWLEDGMENTS

I take this opportunity to thank Dr. David Soren of the University of Missouri–Columbia for suggesting this publication and for help in its preparation; I am grateful also to Dr. Soren and to Dr. Diana Buitron of The Walters Art Gallery, as co-directors of the excavations at Kourion, for permission to study and excavate the planting pits in the sanctuary there. Originally, much of this article was given as a talk at the annual meeting of the American Philological Association in December 1979, for helpful advice concerning which I am indebted to Dr. Stephen G. Miller of the University of California at Berkeley.

Part V

Spuria

CHAPTER 12.

A POSSIBLE LATE CYPRIOTE BOAT MODEL

Albert Leonard, Jr.

Although it has been described as a Late Cypriote or Cypro-Archaic boat model, the acquisition labeled Accession No. U.Mo. 62.32 in the Museum of Art and Archaeology at the University of Missouri-Columbia remains a mystery. Acquired by the Museum in 1962, the object is 20.7 cm long and 7.2 cm wide (Figures 12-1 through 12-3). It is made of a whitish fabric decorated with brownish paint, a description which to many archaeologists working in the eastern Mediterranean calls to mind a specific Late Cypriote fabric: White Slip ware. That the Late Bronze Age Cypriotes were actively engaged in water-borne commerce is well attested in the archaeological record, and, if this were a model of a craft employed in such trade, it would expand present knowledge on a very important subject.

The Cypriote origin and date have been questioned by some visitors in the 17 years this object has been in the Museum, and a wide variety of other dates, proveniences, and functions has been offered. Thus, it was decided to present the piece during the symposium on Cypriote archaeology, and this paper is an interim research report describing the findings to date.

The object's function frequently has been explained as either that of a lamp or a model boat. Its use as a lamp is easy to visualize: oil would simply be poured into the center, a wick added at the end and then lit. Two factors, however, might argue against such an interpretation. Oil poured into the vessel would stain the interior, but absolutely no trace of stain appears. Nor is there any trace of burning around the fractured end of the "nozzle." These two observations do not necessarily prove that the piece was not designed as a lamp, but only suggest that it was never used as one.

The second major interpretation of U.Mo. 62.32 is that of a model boat. For this identification, the prow, foredeck, open cabin, rear deck, steering oar mechanism, and high stern would be noted (right to left fig. 12-1a). The painted and molded decoration could then be understood as real attributes of the vessel, such as lines and stays for the rigging, or intangible attributes, such as the ability to see, and thus avoid, the ever present dangers of the sea.

Perhaps it is not too early in this study to propose a third compromise interpretation, i.e., a votive lamp in the form of a boat. The question remains, however, is it Late Bronze Age Cypriote? An analysis of the decoration may help to determine the vessel's date.

Stated simply, there are basically two major types of Late Cypriote pottery: Base-ring ware and White Slip ware.* They are hand- rather than wheel-made, and the decoration, whether raised or painted, is hand executed in linear or geometric patterns. They lack, therefore, the complex decoration on the foredeck of the Missouri model. It should be kept in mind, however, that the latter part of the Late Bronze Age in Cyprus was a period of intense Mycenaean Greek influence and eventual colonization; while the decoration on Cypriote pottery is basically linear in nature, the Mycenaeans delighted in representational motives and the stylistic abstractions that could be achieved through hybridization.

The primary source for the study of Mycenaean pottery is the pioneer work of the Swedish scholar Arne Furumark, *Mycenaean Pottery: Analysis and Classification* (1941). In his landmark study, Furumark isolated 78 basic motives and their chronological variants. Examples of the five Mycenaean motives most pertinent to the present study are illustrated in Figure 12-4, with the decoration from the Missouri model shown at the bottom. While some similarities do exist and the decoration on the Missouri model does appear to reflect the spirit of the Mycenaean vase painter, the Missouri motive cannot be closely paralleled among the products of either Cypriote or Aegean Late Bronze Age ateliers.

The technique by which this piece was crafted also presents a problem. It was formed in a bipartite mold, the seam between the two halves having been pared down to smooth the junction. Although the technique of "paring" is popular on at least one Late Cypriote juglet form (cf. Åström 1972b:221-225, White Shaved ware; 225-231, Plain White Hand-made ware), the use of the mold is peculiar since both Cypriote and Mycenaean models and figurines were hand-formed. Although the use of the mold can be documented for metal and glass frit, it was not used for terracotta objects.

Since the employment of the mold and the decoration give one pause in assigning the Missouri model to the Late Bronze Age, one also must consider how the piece compares with other boat models of more demonstrably Late Cypriote provenience and date. Actual Late Cypriote boat models are known from funerary contexts at Maroni, Tombs 1 and 7 (Merrillees 1968:188 and pl. 37:2), and Kazaphani, Tomb 2b (Merrillees 1968: 188, illustrated Karageorghis 1964: 336, fig. 70). A fourth, of unknown context, also comes from Enkomi (Merrillees 1968: 188-189, pl. 37:1). All four of these can be generally described as open, canoe-like forms with high prows and sterns, which contrast sharply with the covered fore and afterdecks and almost horizontal prow of the Missouri piece. Some details are indicated on the Maroni and Kazaphani models, but they consist basically of raised lines along the hull, a row of perforations along the gunwales, or simple projections. All these elements can be viewed as attempts at rendering actual, functional features of the crafts which inspired the model vessels. Painted decoration is absent (or not preserved) and, while eyes are depicted on one 7th century ship model (Gray 1974: G31, HH3h, pl. GIV:a), no indication of such a "philosophical" attitude on the part of the Late

---

*For a full discussion of Late Cypriote pottery, see Åström 1972.

Cypriote "Boat"

POTTERY SAMPLE

All values are ppm unless otherwise specified

Ti	.579%
Mg	24.3 mg/g
V	116
Al	11.0%
Mn	1.24 mg/g
Co	30.2
Ta	1.05
Na	1.03%
La	20.8
Ce	50
Lu	.36
Th	4.48
Cr	128
Eu	1.58
Yb	2.05
Au	2.1
Ba	274
*Nd	22
Sr	170
Tb	1.7
Sc	12.6
Rb	<71
Fe	4.30%

*Not supported with quality control.

Table 12-1.

Bronze Age craftsmen is evident. In all, the Missouri model gives the impression of being much more streamlined (and hence more advanced?) than those of definable Cypriote provenience and Late Bronze Age date.

From the very beginning of this study it was felt that consideration of the typological and stylistic elements alone would not be sufficient to solve the problem of the date and origin of the Missouri model. Accordingly, while the typological and stylistic elements were being studied, arrangements were made for a potentially more objective approach to identifying the origin and date of the piece: an analysis of the chemical composition of the clay from which the vessel was fashioned.

The model was sampled by Maura F. Cornman, Conservator of the Museum of Art and Archaeology, and Dr. James Vogt, Director of the Research Reactor Facility at the University of Missouri-Columbia, and was tested by Dr. Vogt and Chris Graham, Senior Research Specialist at the Research Reactor, University of Missouri, by neutron activation analysis. The results of these tests are listed in Table 12-1. Since comparative data on Cypriote White Slipped pottery is yet to be published, Drs. Asaro and Pearlman at the Lawrence Berkeley Laboratory at the University of California, Berkeley, were consulted. The Lawrence Berkeley Laboratory is the major American center conducting such research. Drs. Asaro and Pearlman compared this data, by telephone, with the results of tests they had previously conducted on White Slip vessels found at several Cypriote sites.

They pointed out inter alia the following discrepancies:

1. Scandium

    UMC shows 12.6 ppm compared with Cypriote examples which contain between 35 and 43 ppm.

2. Tantalum

    UMC shows 1.05 ppm while all White Slip tests to approximately 1/3 ppm.

3. Iron

    UMC shows 4.30 percent, which is somewhat lower than the Lawrence results.

The results of the neutron activation test and their comparison with the fabric of White Slip vessels actually excavated in Cyprus would seem to deny Cypriote origin for this piece, an assignment based primarily on the visual appearance of the fabric and paint, the seemingly Mycenaean-inspired decoration on the foredeck, and the existence of other Cypriote boat models. It must, however, be remembered that the stylistic and typological investigation also had raised doubts about the claimed Cypriote pedigree. These doubts were caused by the use of the mold in the construction of the piece and for its decoration, and the fact that the model exhibited only vague similarities to other Late Bronze Age boat representations.

If this little boat-lamp has failed the tests for its Late Bronze Age Cypriote origin and date, must it then be sentenced to remain forever in a state of limbo? Certainly not, for it is the responsibility of anyone working on this type of problem to offer new hypotheses when challenging or dispelling the old.

In early October 1979, Dr. James Sauer, Director of the American Center for Oriental Research in Amman, Jordan, visited the Museum of Art and Archaeology and suggested that the piece might be Arabic rather than Cypriote. Investigation of this possibility has definitely provided an alternative hypothesis.

During the Ummayad period (661-750 A.D.) a minor form of lamp existed termed the "Jerash type" after the important Jordanian site (Day 1942:74-79, compare pls. 13-14 for many similarities between the "Jerash type" lamp and the Missouri model). Not only were many such lamps found at Jerash—although most remain unpublished—but their molds also have been recovered.

All the "Jerash type" lamps share the tall, raised handle with hand-formed tripartite tip (Figure 12-5), but they can vary in other elements. They can have a round ring base or an elongated flat base quite similar to that of the Missouri model. There may or may not be a trough around the filling orifice. Decoration can be either geometric or inscriptional. In fact, the eclectic nature of the Ummayad workshops, as well as the lack of any deep religious conviction on the craftsman's part, is clearly demonstrated on one lamp which juxtaposes a Christian inscription on the top mold and an Ummayad inscription in Kufic Arabic on the bottom mold (Day 1942: pl. 14:1).

Specific decorative elements on the Missouri model's foredeck that can be paralleled on the "Jerash type" lamps include the voluted ribs with dotted fill changing to dotted border, and the concentric rings that are so temptingly interpreted as eyes. In fact, a slightly earlier lamp from Jerash has the representation of a human face in exactly the same position between the filling orifice and the nozzle (Kennedy 1963: pl. 27, 711/20). The pellets on the afterdeck might be considered the vestigial remains of the voluted and concentric rings which appear in this area on some Jerash lamps. Even the painted decoration on the gunwales of the Missouri piece can find possible inspiration in the molded decoration of the "Jerash type" lamp.

The similarity between the Missouri model and the 8th century Jerash lamps is striking and definitely warrants further investigation after fuller publication of the type. The question remains, however, should one entwine oneself again in the Gordion Knot of whether this is a model boat or simply a lamp of the Ummayad period. Alexander's solution to the question would be simple, but not scholarly. One must recall that the Arabs of the Ummayad period were actively engaged in water-borne commerce, as can be seen by the fact that after the capture of Egypt in 641 A.D. a reversal of the hitherto normal East to West trading patterns set in. Thus, until the expedition of Vasco da Gama at the very end of the 15th century, much of Eastern Mediterranean trade previously earmarked for European ports was diverted via the Red Sea to Mecca and Medina.

Nor was this usurpation of the Southeastern Mediterranean trade the end of it, for the western Ummayad expansion continued until, during the Caliphate of Abd al-Malak, the Muslim forces were defeated by Charles Martel near Tours in 732 A.D. This defeat marked the centennial of the Prophet's death as well as the end of Arabic expansion in Europe.

As for the ships that plied the Red Sea trade during the Ummayad period or provided logistical support for their land-based European expansion to the west, there is, unfortunately, little in the way of contemporary pictorial records with which to compare the Missouri model. The similarities betwen it and the "Jerash type" lamp are, however, at least as convincing as those previously used to bolster its Late Bronze Age Cypriote pedigree. Perhaps future comparisons of the chemical composition of the clay will help determine a proper home for this intriguing creation.

Although this study has been unable to offer a definite provenience and date for U.Mo. 62.32, it has at least eliminated Late Bronze Age Cyprus from the contest and suggested the possibility that it might be an almost singular example of an 8th century Ummayad boat. Equally as important, however, is the fact that it has proven once again the value of the arts and sciences working together toward the common goal of reconstructing ancient civilization.

APPENDIX

Following the presentation of Leonard's paper at the symposium in October 1979, the model was tested for its thermoluminescence age by Professor Ralph Rowlett of the University of Missouri-Columbia. The results confirm Leonard's conclusions that the object does not belong to the Late Bronze Age. Considering the problems in testing (see below), the dates arrived at are not too far off the Ummayad period.

The Editors

TL AGE CALCULATION REPORT

MATL #80-1,   Museum of Art and Archaeology   62.32

Environmental radiation estimated at .4 Rads per annum
        (Fleming 1979: 3) since burial context is unknown.

Self-Irradiation _____ Rads per annum

Irradiation dose of ___800___ ± R represents age of __2,000__ years

when the ratio of Original TL to Induced TL is   Sample Eb .990
                                                 Sample Fb .707 .

Error ± ___13_____ % without taking into account the unknown background
                                radiation, so this is a minimal statement.

Average
Calculated age ___1,700 ± 221___ years or A.D. ___280___ ± ___221___ .

The black temper grains, which appeared possibly to be sandstone, but which were basalt, were not susceptible to induced irradiation. Therefore, we used two small pieces of the yellow ceramic fragment. This is not the best approach, ideally, to TL ceramic dating, but, in this case, was the best we had to work with. The age estimations are based on this material. It seems most unlikely that the boat is any older by several centuries, so a Bronze Age date seems unlikely.

Ralph M. Rowlett

ACKNOWLEDGMENTS

Special thanks are due to Doctors Asaro and Pearlman, and to the Lawrence Berkeley Laboratory for their kind cooperation in this study. I should also like to thank Professor Rowlett for his help.

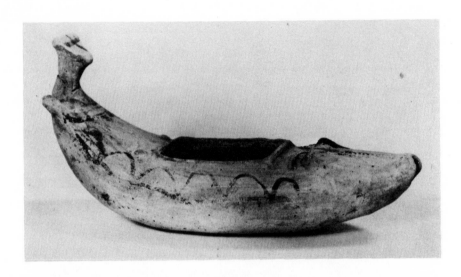

12-1. Terracotta lamp or model, Museum of Art
and Archaeology, University of Missouri-Columbia.
a. side view; b. top view.

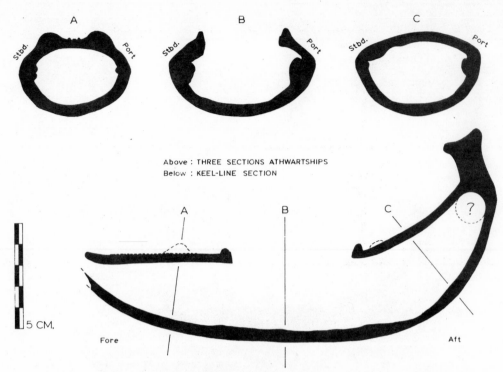

Above : THREE SECTIONS ATHWARTSHIPS
Below : KEEL-LINE SECTION

5 CM.

12-2. Sections through terracotta lamp or boat model. Drawn by John Huffstot.

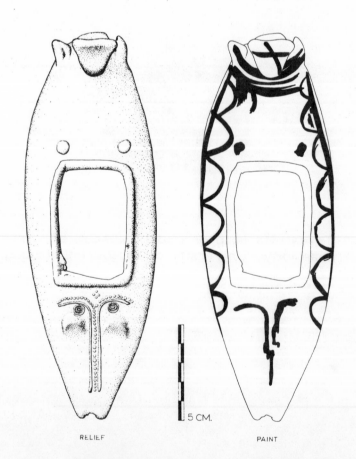

RELIEF

5 CM.

PAINT

12-3. Decoration on the terracotta lamp or boat model. Drawn by John Huffstot.

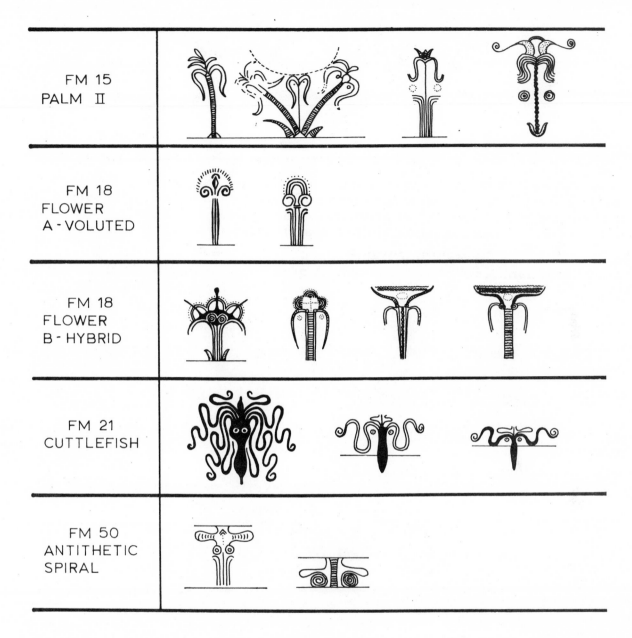

FM 15 PALM II	
FM 18 FLOWER A - VOLUTED	
FM 18 FLOWER B - HYBRID	
FM 21 CUTTLEFISH	
FM 50 ANTITHETIC SPIRAL	

U. MO. 62.32

12-4. Mycenaean motives and decoration on the Missouri model. Mycenaean motives from Furumark 1941, reproduced by permission.

12-5.   Terracotta lamp of "Jerash
type," Museum of Art and Archaeology, University of Missouri-
Columbia (U.Mo. 64.35). a. side
view; b. top view.

Bibliography

BIBLIOGRAPHY

List of Abbreviations

AJA:	*American Journal of Archaeology*
AthMitt:	*Mitteilungen des deutschen Archäologischen Instituts, Athenische Abteilung*
BASOR:	*Bulletin of the American Schools of Oriental Research*
BCH:	*Bulletin de correspondance héllenique*
BICS:	*Bulletin of the Institute of Classical Studies of the University of London*
BSA:	*British School at Athens, Annual*
CRAI:	*Comptes rendus de l'Académie des inscriptions et belles lettres*
IG:	*Inscriptiones Graecae*
ILN:	*Illustrated London News*
JFA:	*Journal of Field Archaeology*
JHS:	*Journal of Hellenic Studies*
JRS:	*Journal of Roman Studies*
MAAR:	*Memoirs of the American Academy in Rome*
ProcPhilSoc:	*Proceedings of the American Philosophical Society*
RDAC:	*Report of the Department of Antiquities, Cyprus*
SCE:	*Swedish Cyprus Expedition*
SIMA:	*Studies in Mediterranean Archaeology*
TAPS:	*Transactions of the American Philosophical Society*

ADOVASIO, J.M., G.F. FRY, J.D. GUNN and R.F. MAZLOWSKI
1974   **Prehistoric** and historic settlement patterns in western Cyprus. *World Archaeology* 6:339-364.

ALBENDA, P.
1976   Landscape bas-reliefs in the Bīt-Hilāni of Ashurbanipal. BASOR 224:49-72.

AMBRASEYS, N.N.
1960   *Seismic History of Cyprus* (Imperial Collection of Science and Technology of London University). London: University of London Press.

1965   A note on the seismicity of the eastern Mediterranean. *Studia Geophysica et Geologica* 9(4):405-410.

AMIET, P.
1968   Antiquités iraniennes récemment acquises par le Musée du Louvre. *Syria* 45:249-262.

ÅSTRÖM, P.
    1957   *The Middle Cypriote Bronze Age.* Lund: Hakan
             Ohlssons Boktrycheri.

    1966   *Excavations at Kalopsidha and Ayios Iakovos in Cyprus*
             (SIMA 2). Lund: G.W.K. Gleerup.

    1972a   *The Middle Cypriote Bronze Age* (SCE 4:1B).
             Lund: Swedish Cyprus Expedition.

    1972b   *The Late Cypriote Bronze Age. Architecture and Pottery*
             (SCE 4:1C). Lund: Swedish Cyprus Expedition.

ÅSTRÖM, P. and L.
    1972c   *The Late Cypriote Bronze Age. Relative and Absolute
             Chronology, Foreign Relations, Historical Conclusions*
             (SCE 4:1D). Lund: Swedish Cyprus Expedition.

ÅSTRÖM, P.
    1972d   Some aspects of the Late Cypriote I period. RDAC: 46–57.

ÅSTRÖM, P., J. BIERS, and Others
    1978   *The Cypriote Collection of the Museum of Art and Archaeology,
             University of Missouri-Columbia. Corpus of Cypriote Antiquities*
             (SIMA 20(2)). Gothenburg: Paul Åströms Förlag.

BARNETT, R.D.
    1975   *A Catalogue of the Nimrud Ivories* (2nd edition).
             London: Trustees of the British Museum.

    1977   The Amathus shield-boss rediscovered and the Amathus bowl
             reconsidered. RDAC: 157–169.

BENTON, S.
    1953   Further excavations at Aetos. BSA 48:255–361.

BESQUES, S.
    1936   L'Apollon Μαγείριος de Chypre. *Revue archéologique* (1):3–11.

BIELINSKI, P.
    1974   A prism-shaped stamp seal in Warsaw and related stamps.
             Berytus 23:53–69.

BISI, A.M.
    1962   L'Iconografia del grifone a Cipro. *Oriens Antiquus* 1:219–232.

BLINKENBERG, C.
    1931   *Lindos, fouilles de l'Acropole, 1902–1914,* Vol. 1.
             Berlin: Walter de Gruyter and Cie.

BOARDMAN, J.
    1961/62 Ionian bronze belts. *Anatolia* 6:179–189.

1967 *Chios: Excavations in Emporio* (BSA Supplement
6). Cambridge: University Press.

BROADHEAD, H.D.
 1960 *The Persae of Aeschylus.* Cambridge: University Press.

BROWN, W.L.
 1960 *The Etruscan Lion.* Oxford: Clarendon Press.

BUCHHOLZ, H.-G. and V. KARAGEORGHIS
 1973 *Prehistoric Greece and Cyprus.* London: Phaidon Press.

BUITRON, D. and D. SOREN
 1979 Missouri in Cyprus: the Kourion expedition. MUSE 13:22-31.

CATLING, H.W.
 1962 Patterns of settlement in Bronze Age Cyprus.
Opuscula Atheniensia 4:129-169.

 1971 Cyprus in the Early Bronze Age, in I.E.S. Edwards,
C.J. Gadd, N.G.L. Hammond, eds., *The Cambridge
Ancient History* (3rd edition), Vol. 1 (2), 802-823.
Cambridge: University Press.

CESNOLA, L. PALMA DI
 1877 *Cyprus: Its Ancient Cities, Tombs and Temples.*
New York: Harper and Brothers.

CHANTRAINE, P.
 1968 *Dictionnaire étymologique de la langue grecque.*
Paris: Klincksieck.

CHRISTOFIDOU, M.K.
 1969-72 Οἱ σεισμοὶ καὶ αἱ σεισμικαὶ δονήσεις ἐν Κύπρῳ ἀπὸ τῆς
ἀρχαιότητος μέχρι σήμερον. Κυπριακὸς Λόγος 4:22-270 ff.

COLEMAN, J.E.
 1977 Cornell excavations at Alambra, 1976. RDAC: 71-79.

COLEMAN, J.E. and J.A. BARLOW
 1979 Cornell excavations at Alambra, 1978. RDAC: 159-167.

COLONNA-CECCALDI, G.
 1882 *Monuments antiques de Chypre, de Syrie et d'Égypte.*
Paris: Didier.

CONRAD, D.
 1971 Der Gott Reschef. *Zeitschrift für Alttestamentliche
Wissenschaft* 83: 157-183.

COOK, A.B.
 1925 *Zeus. A Study in Ancient Religion,* Vol. 2. Cambridge:
University Press.

COX, D.H.
1959   *Coins from the Excavations at Curium 1932-1953*
(Numismatic Notes and Monographs 145). New York:
American Numismatic Society.

CULICAN, W.
1968   The iconography of some Phoenician seals and seal
impressions. *Australian Journal of Biblical Archaeology*
1:50-103.

1977   Syrian and Cypriote cubical seals. *Levant* 9:162-167.

CURIUM (no author listed)
1961   *A Brief History and Description of Curium.*
Nicosia: Anagennis Press.

CURTIS, C.D.
1919   The Bernardini Tomb. MAAR 3:9-90.

CURTIUS, E., F. ADLER and G. HIRSCHFELD
1966   *Olympia*, Vol. 4 (reprint of 1878 edition). Amsterdam:
Adolf M. Hakkert.

CURTIUS G.
1875-76 *Principles of Greek Etymology* (trans A. Wilkins and
E. England). London: J. Murray.

DANTHINE, H.
1937   *Le Palmier-dattier et les arbres sacrées* (Bibliothèque
archéologique et historique 25). Paris: Librairie
orientaliste Paul Geuthner.

DAY, F.E.
1942   Early Islamic and Christian Lamps. *Berytus* 7:65-79.

DEECKE, W.
1886   Zu den epichorischen kyprischen Inschriften. *Beiträge zur
Kunde der indogermanischen Sprachen* 11:315-319.

DIKAIOS, P.
1936   The excavations at Erimi, 1933-35:final report. RDAC: 1-81.

1946   Early Copper Age discoveries in Cyprus: 3rd millennium B.C.
copper mining. ILN 208:244-245.

1960   A conspectus of architecture in ancient Cyprus.
Kypriakai Spoudai 24:1-30.

1961   *Sotira* (Museum monographs). Philadelphia: University Museum.

1962   *The Stone Age* (SCE 4:1A) 1-204. Lund: Swedish Cyprus
Expedition.

1969a   *Enkomi: Excavations 1948–1958,* Vol. 1, *Architectural remains. Tombs.* Mainz: P. von Zabern.

1969b   *Enkomi: Excavations 1948–1958,* Vol. 3 *Plates.* Mainz: P. von Zabern.

DURYEA, D.

1965   The Necropolis of Phaneromeni and its Relations to Other Early Bronze Age Sites in Cyprus. M.A. thesis. University of Missouri-Columbia.

DUSSAUD, R.

1934   Ceinture en bronze du Louristan avec scènes de chasse. *Syria* 15:187–199.

1949   Anciens bronzes du Louristan et cultes iraniens. *Syria* 26:196–229.

ELLIOTT, G. and R. DUTTON

1963   *Know Your Rocks, An Introduction to Geology in Cyprus.* Nicosia: Zavallis Press.

FLEMING, S.

1979   *Thermoluminescence Techniques in Archaeology.* Oxford: Clarendon Press.

FRANKEL, D.

1974   *Middle Cypriot White Painted Pottery* (SIMA 42). Göteborg: Paul Åströms Förlag.

FRANKEN, H.J.

1971   Analysis of methods of potmaking in archaeology. *Harvard Theological Review* 64:227–255.

FRANKFORT, H.

1970   *Art and Architecture of the Ancient Orient* (4th edition revised). Middlesex: Penguin Books.

FRASER, P.M.

1972   *Ptolemaic Alexandria,* Vols. 1–3. Oxford: Clarendon Press.

FRISK, H.

1960   *Griechisches etymologisches Wörterbuch.* Heidelberg: C. Winter.

FURUMARK, A.

1941   *Mycenaean Pottery I, Analysis and Classification* (Acta Instituti Atheniensis Regni Sueciae 4°, 20). Stockholm (1972 reprint of the original publication).

GALLET DE SANTERRE, H. and J. TRÉHEUX

1974   Rapport sur le dépôt égéen et géométrique de l'Artémision à Délos. BCH 71:148–254.

GARDNER, E.A., D.G. HOGARTH and M.R. JAMES
    1888   Excavations in Cyprus, 1887–1888. Paphos, Leontari, Amargetti, VI Inscriptions of Kuklia and Amargetti. JHS 9:225–263.

GARDNER, E.A.
    1888   *Naukratis II* (Sixth Memoir of the Egypt Exploration Fund). London: Trubner and Co.

GJERSTAD, E.
    1926   *Studies on Prehistoric Cyprus*. Uppsala: A.B. Lundequistska.

GJERSTAD, E., E. LINDROS, E. SJÖQVIST and A. WESTHOLM
    1937   *Finds and Results of the Excavations in Cyprus 1927–1931* (SCE 3). Stockholm: The Swedish Cyprus Expedition.

GJERSTAD, E.
    1948   *The Cypro-Geometric, Cypro-Archaic, and Cypro-Classical Periods* (SCE 4:2). Stockholm: Swedish Cyprus Expedition.

GRAY, D.
    1974   *Seewesen* (Archaeologia Homerica. Im Auftrage des deutschen Archäologischen Instituts), F. Matz and H.-G. Buchholz eds. Göttingen: Vandenhoeck and Ruprecht.

GUTHRIE, W.K.C.
    1951   *The Greeks and their Gods*. Boston: Beacon Press.

HARTWELL, K.
    1922   Nature in Theocritus. *Classical Journal* 17(4):181–190.

HELLBING, L.
    1979   *Alasia Problems* (SIMA 57). Göteborg: Paul Åströms Förlag.

HERSCHER, E.
    1973   Red-and-black polished ware from the western Karpas. RDAC: 62–71.

    1976   South coast ceramic styles at the end of Middle Cypriote. RDAC: 11–19.

    1978   The Bronze Age Cemetery at Lapithos, Vrysi Tou Barba, Cyprus. Results of the University of Pennsylvania Museum Excavation, 1931. Doctoral dissertation, University of Pennsylvania.

HILL, P.V., R.A.G. CARSON, and J.P.C. KENT
    1965   *Late Roman Bronze Coinage*. London: Spink and Son.

HOFFMANN, O.
    1899   Etymologien in A. Bezzenberger and W. Prellwitz, eds., *Beiträge zur Kunde der indogermanischen Sprachen* 25, 106–109. Göttingen: R. Peppmüller.

HOFMANN, J.
    1950   *Etymologisches Wörterbuch des Griechischen.*
                Munich: R. Oldenbourg.

HOGARTH, D.G.
    1888   Excavations in Cyprus, 1887-88. Paphos, Leontari,
                Amargetti, I. The first season's work. Preliminary
                narrative. JHS 9:149-174.

    1889   *Devia Cypria: Notes of an Archaeological Journey in Cyprus
                in 1888.* London: Henry Frowde.

KARAGEORGHIS, V.
    1940-48   Finds from Early Cypriot cemeteries. RDAC: 115-152.

    1960   Chronique des fouilles et découvertes archéologiques
                à Chypre en 1959. BCH 84:242-299.

    1964   Chronique des fouilles et découvertes archéologiques à
                Chypre en 1963. BCH 88:289-379.

    1965a   Chronique des fouilles et découvertes archéologiques à
                Chypre en 1964. BCH 89:231-300.

    1965b   *Nouveaux documents pour l'étude du Bronze récent à Chypre.*
                Paris: E. de Boccard.

    1973a   Chronique des fouilles et découvertes archéologiques à
                Chypre en 1972. BCH 97:601-689.

    1973b   *Excavations in the Necropolis of Salamis,* III (Salamis 5).
                Nicosia: Zavallis Press.

    1976   Chronique des fouilles et découvertes archéologiques à
                Chypre en 1975. BCH 100:839-906.

    1977   Chronique des fouilles et découvertes archéologiques à
                Chypre en 1976. BCH 101:707-779.

    1978a   Chronique des fouilles et découvertes archéologiques à
                Chypre en 1977. BCH 102:879-938.

    1978b   A "Favissa" at Kazaphani. RDAC: 156-193.

    1979   Chronique des fouilles et découvertes archéologiques à
                Chypre en 1978. BCH 103:671-724.

    1980   Fouilles à l'ancienne Paphos de Chypre: les premiers colons
                Achéens. CRAI: 122-136.

KENNEDY, C.A.
    1963   The development of the lamp in Palestine. *Berytus* 14:67-115.

KESHISHIAN, K.K.
    1977   *Romantic Cyprus.* Nicosia: Printco.

KROMHOLZ, S.F.
    1979   The ceramics of Kalavasos-Tenta, in I.A. Todd et al.,
             Vasilikos Valley project, 1977-1978: an interim report.
             RDAC: 35-39.

LANG, R.H.
    1878   Narrative of excavations in a temple at Dali (Idalion).
             Transactions of the Royal Society of Literature, 2nd ser.,
             11:30-71.

LAST, J.
    1975   Kourion: The ancient water supply. ProcPhilSoc 119(1):39-72.

LIDDELL, H. and R. SCOTT
    1968   *A Greek-English Lexicon.* Oxford: Clarendon Press.

MCFADDEN, G.
    1935-53 Field Diary. Unpublished.

    1938   The sanctuary of Apollo. *University Museum Bulletin* 7:10-17.

    1940   The sanctuary of Apollo at Kourion. *University Museum
             Bulletin* 8:22-28.

    1950   Kourion - The Apollo Baths. *University Museum Bulletin*
             14:14-26.

    1951   Cyprus. AJA 55:167-168.

    1952a   Cyprus, 1950-51. AJA 56:128-129.

    1952b   Eleven hundred years of the worship of Apollo of the
             Woodlands. ILN 220:588-590.

MAIER, F.G.
    1975   The temple of Aphrodite at Old Paphos. RDAC:69-80.

MALLOWAN, M.E.L.
    1966   *Nimrud and its Remains,* Vol. 2. New York: Dodd, Mead and Co.

MARTIN, R.
    1976   Bathyclès de Magnésie et le 'trône' d'Apollon à Amyklae.
             Revue archéologique (2):205-218.

MASSON, O.
    1960a   Notes épigraphiques II, Apollon Λακευτής· *Glotta* 39:112-114.

    1960b   Cultes indigènes, cultes grecs et cultes orientaux à Chypre.
             Éléments orientaux dans la religion grecque ancienne (Colloque
             de Strasbourg 22-24 mai 1958), 129-142. Paris: Presses
             universitaires de France.

1961   *Les Inscriptions chypriotes syllabiques.* Paris: E. de Boccard.

1966   Kypriaka II. Recherches sur les antiquités de la région de Pyla. <u>BCH</u> 90:1-21.

1968   Kypriaka VII. Le Sanctuaire d'Apollon à Idalion. <u>BCH</u> 92:386-402.

MENARDOS, S.
1906   Τοπωνυμικὸν τῆς Κύπρου. ᾿Αθηνᾶ 18:315-421.

MERRILLEES, R.S.
1966   Finds from Kalopsidha Tomb 34 , in P. Åström, *Excavations at Kalopsidha and Ayios Iakovos in Cyprus* (SIMA 2) 31-37. Lund: Carl Bloms.

1968   *The Cypriote Bronze Age Pottery Found in Egypt* (SIMA 18). Lund: Paul Åströms Förlag.

1971   The early history of Late Cypriote I. *Levant* 3:56-79.

1978   *Introduction to the Bronze Age Archaeology of Cyprus* (SIMA Pocket-book 9). Göteborg: Paul Åströms Förlag.

MILLER, R.D.
1939   The Origin and Original Nature of Apollo. Doctoral dissertation, University of Pennsylvania.

MILNE, J.G.
1901   Greek Inscriptions from Egypt. <u>JHS</u> 21:275-292.

MITFORD, T.B.
1946   Religious documents from Roman Cyprus. <u>JHS</u> 66:24-42.

1960a   Paphian inscriptions Hoffmann nos. 98 and 99. <u>BICS</u> 7:1-10.

1960b   A Cypriot oath of allegiance to Tiberius. <u>JRS</u> 50:75-79.

1961   Further contributions to the epigraphy of Cyprus. <u>AJA</u> 65:93-151.

1971   *The Inscriptions of Kourion* (Memoirs of the American Philosophical Society). Philadelphia: American Philosophical Society.

MOOREY, P.R.S.
1967   Some ancient metal belts: their antecedents and relatives. *Iran* 5:83-98.

MYRES, J.L.
1914   *Handbook of the Cesnola Collection.* New York: Metropolitan Museum of Art.

NICOLAOU, I.
1969   Inscriptiones Cypriae alphabeticae VIII, 1968. <u>RDAC</u>: 71-94.

OATES, D.
1959   Fort Shalmaneser - An interim report. *Iraq* 21:98-129.

OHNEFALSCH-RICHTER, M.
1893   *Kypros, the Bible, and Homer*. London: Asher.

ORTHMANN, W.
1971   *Untersuchungen zur späthethitischen Kunst*. Bonn: Rudolph Habelt.

OVERBECK, J.C. and S. SWINY
1972   *Two Cypriot Bronze Age sites at Kafkallia (Dhali)* (SIMA 33). Göteborg: Paul Åströms Förlag.

PAGE, D.L.
1959   *Sappho and Alcaeus*. Oxford: Clarendon Press.

PALLOTTINO, M.
1975   *The Etruscans* (trans J. Cremona), D. Ridgway, ed. Bloomington: Indiana University Press.

PAYNE, H.
1931   *Necrocorinthia*. Oxford: Clarendon Press.

PELTENBURG, E.J.
1977   Chalcolithic figurine from Lemba, Cyprus. *Antiquity* 51:140-143.

1978   The Sotira culture: regional diversity and cultural unity in Late Neolithic Cyprus. *Levant* 10:55-74.

1979   Lemba archaeological project, Cyprus 1976-77: preliminary report. *Levant* 11:9-45.

PERISTIANES, I.K.
1910   <u>Γενικὴ ἱστορία τῆς νήσου Κύπρου ἀπὸ τῶν ἀρχαιοτάτων χρόνων μέχρι τῆς Ἀγγλικῆς κατοχῆς</u>. Λευκοσία: φωνὴ τῆς Κύπρου.

PARROT, A.
1958   Acquisitions et inédits du Musée du Louvre. *Syria* 35:163-186.

POKORNY, J.
1959   *Indogermanisches etymologisches Wörterbuch*, Vol. 1. Bern: Francke.

PORADA, E.
1979   A Theban cylinder seal in Cypriote style with Minoan elements, in *The Relations between Cyprus and Crete, ca. 2000-500 B.C.* (Acts of the International Archaeological Symposium, Nicosia, April 16-22, 1978): 111-120. Nicosia: Chr. Nicolaou & Sons.

POTRATZ, J.A.H.
   1964   Das Flechtband. Eine altvorderasiatische Ligatur.
             Oriens Antiquus 3:175-220.

POULSEN, F.
   1912   *Der Orient und die frühgriechische Kunst.* Leipzig: B. Teubner.

PRELLWITZ, W.
   1892   *Etymologisches Wörterbuch des griechischen Sprache.*
             Göttingen: Vandenhoek and Ruprecht.

ROBERT, L.
   1978   Sur un Apollon oraculaire à Chypre.   CRAI:338-344.

ROSENMEYER, T.G.
   1969   *The Green Cabinet.* Berkeley: University of California Press.

SAKELLARIOS, A.A.
   1890   Τὰ Κυπριακὰ ἤτοι γεωγραφία ἱστορία καὶ γλῶσσα
             τῆς νήσου Κύπρου ἀπὸ τῶν ἀρχαιοτάτων
             χρόνων μέχρι σήμερον,   Vol 1. Athens: P.D. Sakellarios.

SCHMIDT, G.
   1968   *Kyprische Bildwerke aus dem Heraion von Samos* (Samos 7).
             Bonn: Rudolf Habelt.

SCRANTON, R.
   1967   The architecture of the sanctuary of Apollo Hylates at
             Kourion. TAPS 57(5):3-85.

SJÖQVIST, E.
   1933   Die Kultgeschichte eines cyprischen Temenos. *Archiv für
             Religionswissenschaft* 30:308-359.

SNELL, B. and H. METTE
   1955   *Lexikon der frühgriechischen Epos.* Göttingen: Vandenhoek
             and Ruprecht.

SOREN, D.
   1979   The temple of Apollo at the sanctuary of Apollo Hylates.
             RDAC: 321-327.

STANLEY PRICE, N.P.
   1979   The structure of settlement at Sotira in Cyprus.
             Levant 11:46-83.

STEWART, E. and J.R.
   1950   *Vounous 1937-38* (Acta Instituti Romani Regni Sueciae 14).
             Lund: C.W.K. Gleerup.

STEWART, J.
   1978   Preliminary remarks on the Chalcolithic pottery
             wares from Lemba Lakkous. RDAC: 8-19.

STEWART, J.R.
1962   *The Early Cypriote Bronze Age* (SCE 4:1A) 205-391. Lund: Swedish Cyprus Expedition.

STILLWELL, R.
1961   Kourion: the theater. ProcPhilSoc 105:37-78.

STUPKA, D.
1972   *Der Gurtel in der griechischen Kunst.* Dissertation, Universität Wien.

SUTHERLAND, C.H.V. and R.A.G. CARSON, eds.
1966   *Roman Imperial Coinage*, Vol. 7. London: Spink and Son.

SWINY, S.
1976   Stone "offering tables" from Episkopi Phaneromeni. RDAC: 43-56.

1979   Southern Cyprus, 2000-1500 B.C. Doctoral dissertation, University of London, Institute of Archaeology.

1980   Bronze Age gaming stones from Cyprus. RDAC (in press).

1981   Bronze Age settlement patterns in southwest Cyprus. *Levant* 13 (in press).

TATTON-BROWN, V., ed.
1979   *Cyprus B.C. 7000 Years of History.* London: British Museum Publications.

TODD, I.A.
1977a   Vasilikos Valley project: first preliminary report, 1976. RDAC: 5-32.

1977b   The Vasilikos Valley project, 1976. JFA 4:375-381.

1978   Excavations at Kalavasos-Tenta, Cyprus. *Archaeology* 31(4):58-59.

In press A Cypriote Neolithic Wall-Painting. *Antiquity*.

TODD, I.A. et al.
1978   Vasilikos Valley project: second preliminary report, 1977. JFA 5:161-195.

1979a   Vasilikos Valley project, 1977-1978: an interim report. RDAC: 13-68.

1979b   Vasilikos Valley project: third preliminary report, 1978. JFA 6:265-300.

USSISHKIN, D.
1972   A neo-Hittite base from Cyprus. *Archaeology* 25:304-305.

VIERNEISEL, K. and H. WALTER
1959   Ägyptische und orientalische Funde aus Brennen G und dem Bothros. AthMitt 74:35-42.

WEINBERG, S.S.
    1956   Exploring the Early Bronze Age in Cyprus.
                Archaeology 9:112-121.

    1981   *Bamboula at Kourion: The Architecture* (University Museum
                Monographs 42). Philadelphia: University Museum (in press).

WESTHOLM, A.
    1933   The Paphian temple of Aphrodite. *Acta Archaeologica* 4:201-236.

WILSON, V.
    1975   The iconography of Bes with particular reference to the
                Cypriot evidence. *Levant* 7:77-103.

YADIN, Y.
    1977   "Megiddo", Michael Avi-Yonah and Ephraim Stern, eds.,
                in *Encyclopedia of Archaeological Excavations in the Holy Land*,
                Vol. 3, 830-856. Oxford: University Press.

YON, M.
    1973   Les Lions archaïque, *Anthologie Salaminienne* (Salamine de
                Chypre 4, Institut F. Courby). Paris: E. de Boccard.

YOUNG, J. and S.
    1955   *Terracotta Figurines from Kourion in Cyprus* (University
                Museum Monographs). Philadelphia: University Museum.

YOUNG, R.S.
    1957   Gordion 1956: preliminary report.   AJA 61:319-331.

CLASSICAL SOURCES

AELIAN

1959   *Aelian: On the Characteristics of Animals,* (De Natura animalium), A.F. Scholfield, ed. London: W. Heinemann.

AESCHYLUS

1937   *Aeschyli Septem quae Supersunt Tragoediae,* G. Murray, ed. Oxford: Clarendon Press.

1960   *The Persae of Aeschylus,* H.D. Broadhead, ed. Cambridge: University Press.

ARISTOTLE

1831   *Aristotelis Opera,* J. Bekker, ed. Berlin: G. Reiner.

BACCHYLIDES

1970   *Bacchylides,* H. Maehler, ed., revised by B. Snell. Leipzig: B. Teubner.

EURIPIDES

1909   *Euripidis Fabulae,* G. Murray, ed. Oxford: Clarendon Press.

HESYCHIUS

1953   *Hesychii Alexandrini Lexicon,* K. Latte, ed. Copenhagen: E. Munksgaard.

HOMER

1919   *Homeri Opera,* T.W. Allen, ed., Vols. 3 and 4. Oxford: Clarendon Press.

1920   *Homeri Opera,* D.B. Monro and T.W. Allen, eds., Vols. 1 and 2. Oxford: University Press.

HOMERIC HYMN TO APOLLO

1936   *The Homeric Hymns,* T.W. Allen, W.R. Halliday, E.E. Sikes, eds. Oxford: University Press.

LIBANIUS

1979   *The Orations of Libanius,* (Loeb Classical Library) A.F. Norman, ed., Vol. 2. Cambridge: Harvard University Press.

LYCOPHRON

1958   *Alexandra.* E. Scheer, ed., 2 vols. Berlin: Weidmann.

PAUSANIAS

1903   *Graeciae descriptio.* F. Spiro, ed., 3 vols. Leipzig: B. Teubner.

PINDAR

1947   *Pindari Carmina,* C.M. Bowra, ed. Oxford: Clarendon Press.

STEPHANOS OF BYZANTIUM

1958   *Stephan von Byzanz: Ethnika,* A. Meineke, ed. Graz: Akademische Druck-und Verlagsanstalt.

STRABO
    1929   *The Geography* (Loeb Classical Library), T.E. Page, E. Capps and W.H.D. Rouse, eds. London: William Heinemann; New York: G.P. Putnam's Sons.

THEOCRITUS
    1971   *Theocritus: Select Poems*, K.J. Dover, ed. London: Macmillan.

TZETZES
    1908   *Lycophronis Alexandra*, E. Scheer, ed., Vol. 2. Berlin: Weidmann.